Also available

Eat, Drink, and Be Merry
Stand Still and Consider

A Lamp on a Lampstand
A Study of the Parables of Jesus

By Lucas Doremus

To my family,

In Him was life; and the life was the light of men. And the light shines in the darkness, and the darkness did not comprehend it...

That was the true Light which gives light to every man coming into the world.

Introduction

When researching what a parable is, there is general agreement among commentators that it is some kind of figure of speech that compares two things to teach a truth. However, there is much less agreement when it comes to what a parable is not; there is not a clear line of distinction between other figures of speech that are comparisons, such as metaphors and analogies.

In chapters one and two, I explain what I believe is the best definition of what is a parable and what is not a parable. This was informed by research into other teachers and philosophers in the ancient world as well as research into other figures of speech the ancient Greeks defined. Depending on which research is followed, scholars have identified at least 250 types of figures of speech. This is a vast number and, although possible, I doubt the ancient Greek world understood figures of speech in such a meticulous way. Even we in the modern day do not recognize so many figures of speech in normal life even though scholars may do so.

Christian doctrine does not rise and fall on the definition of parable because we can still understand what Jesus is teaching whether we categorize His sayings as parables or not. I think a case could be made that the only parables in the Bible are sections of text defined as parables. However, parables were a common figure of speech and teaching tool among the ancient world. We should be able to recognize a parable because of its form and use rather than being explicitly told in the text a parable is being used.

The best approach to defining parables in the Bible is looking at the sections of text in which we are told a parable is being used and develop a definition from those examples. Then we can look at the rest of the Gospels and see if the same parable form is present elsewhere. We find that Jesus used parables often in His teaching.

I have tried my best to determine which parts of Jesus' sayings are parables and applied those formats to other sayings to build my definition of what a parable is and is not. I looked at how parables begin and end, the comparison that is being made, how Jesus uses them within discourses, how He expected His audience to respond, and how parables are used in groups. I believe the best definition of a parable is *a comparison of a hypothetical situation to reality emphasizing one similarity to enhance a teaching*. I am far from dogmatic about this definition, but having a good definition helps us understand what Jesus was trying to teach and how to understand it.

Whether I am right or wrong in all cases about which teachings are parables and which ones are not, we can still learn together about Jesus' sayings and how to apply them to our lives. I hope we can both grow in grace and knowledge of our Lord and Savior Jesus Christ together through this study (I Peter 3:18).

Chapter 1

What is a Parable?

The word translated "parable" in our English Bible is the Greek word *parabolē*. The Greek word is a compound word: *para* means "alongside" and *bolē* means "to throw." Put together, *parabolē* literally means "to throw alongside." Ultimately, the word carried the meaning of "comparison." Simply put, a parable is a comparison.

Strong's defines *parabolē* as "a similitude, i.e. a fictitious narrative, apothegm or adage" while Vine's says a *parabolē* "signifies 'a placing of one thing beside another' with a view to comparison." Both of these definitions carry the idea of comparison, which is the meaning of the Greek word.

Parabolē is also translated "proverb" (Luke 4:30), "symbolic" (Hebrews 9:9), and "figurative" (Hebrews 11:19). Even though in these cases *parabolē* is not translated "parable," each verse carries the idea of comparing two things, such as the people of Nazareth comparing Jesus to a physician in Luke 4:23. Proverbs, which are short maxims or sayings, can be comparisons though not all are.

In Mark 4:30, Jesus asks, "To what shall we liken the kingdom of God? Or with what parable shall we picture it?" A parable creates a picture in the mind of the hearer. The picture is a hypothetical situation or something that is not reality but could happen in the real world. Creating a picture out of a hypothetical situation reinforces the doctrine the teacher is teaching.

To sum all of this up, a parable is *a comparison of a hypothetical situation to reality emphasizing one similarity to enhance a teaching.* This idea will be developed further in the next chapter.

By my count there are 53 parables in the Gospels because these comparisons follow the definition of a parable and fit the purpose of parables (Matthew 13:10-17) which we will explain in chapter three. While there are different styles a parable can take, all parables share some similarities. Most obviously, all parables will have a prompt that deems a comparison necessary and an audience. All parables compare a hypothetical situation to reality. Parables also only have one meaning; we know this because when Jesus gives us the meaning, which He does for most parables, He only ever gives one.

When talking about the meaning of a parable, instead of using the term "interpretation," I prefer to use the term "provoked thought." In some cases we do have to "interpret" a parable, such as the parable of the sower in which Jesus assigns meaning to the details of the comparison. However, the meaning of the parable isn't necessarily an "interpretation," but rather a "provoked thought" in which the audience is supposed to make a connection between the two things being compared.

There are also similarities that not all parables have but are common throughout the Gospels. Many times parables are told in groups, giving different aspects or details of a theme. Parables can use the same illustration but have a different provoked thought, such as the parable of the lamp on a lampstand (Luke 8:16 and Mark 4:21 vs. Luke 11:33). Jesus probably retold many of His parables, sometimes with slightly different words or details; an example is the parable of the master and the thief. When we see slight differences, it could be the Gospel writers were recording different tellings of the same parable.

Chapter 2

What is Not a Parable?

While defining what a parable is is relatively easy, defining what a parable is not is much more difficult. After looking at research of those who have studied the subject of parables far more than I, there doesn't seem to be a consensus on what a parable is not. Comparing a parable to a metaphor and other figures of speech is one step that will help us.

The Greek word for metaphor is *metaphora* which is a compound word; *meta* means "between" and *phora* is from a root word meaning "to carry." Put together, *metaphora* literally means "to carry over." *Metaphora* came to mean "a transfer."

If we compare the Greek word *parabolē* (literally "to throw alongside") to *metaphora* (literally "to carry over"), both words relate two things together, but *metaphora* is a more direct comparison. A *metaphora* says whatever two things are being compared are the same in whatever aspect is the focus. One thing "carries over" or "transfers" the aspects of itself to the other. Many times there is more than one aspect that is the same which makes the *metaphora* even more powerful. On the other hand, a *parabolē* compares two things that share qualities, but emphasizes one thing in common. A *parabolē* will "throw alongside" or "compare" that one aspect between the two things. Therefore, one thing a *parabolē* is not is a comparison of two things in which qualities can transferred from one to the other. A *parabolē* uses only a single similarity between situations being compared.

An example of a *metaphora* would be Jesus' comparison of Himself with the door of the sheep pen and a shepherd in John 10:1-18. There are many aspects of this comparison that "carry over" the qualities of a door and a shepherd to the identity of Jesus.

There is sometimes a thin line between a *parabolē* and a *metaphora*. Teachers do not teach in strict figures of speech but rather are fluid when making their points. Figures of speech that are hybrids of metaphors and parables, such as the comparison of good trees to people in Matthew 7:16, certainly exist. In this comparison, Jesus creates a hypothetical situation that makes the comparison a *parabolē*. But He concludes the parable by saying, "Therefore, by their fruits you will know them" (Matthew 7:20). This makes the comparison sound more like a *metaphora* because the qualities of fruit and trees are "carried over" to people and their words. Even though this comparison and some others could be argued to be a *metaphora* instead of a *parabolē*, I believe these figures of speech are hybrids of the two. I've included hybrid figures of speech such as these in this book because they follow the parable format even though they have additional figures of speech within the teaching.

An analogy is another figure of speech that compares two things. The Greek word is *analogia*. It is also a compound word: *ana* means "upon, according to" and *logia* is from a root word meaning "ratio." Put together, *analogia* means "proportion." An analogy transfers information or meaning from one thing to another. The two things aren't necessarily being compared to a point of similarity between them. Furthermore, analogies transfer the meaning from one real thing to another whereas a parable compares a hypothetical situation to reality with one point of similarity.

Another figure of speech is a hyperbole. *Hyperbole* is the Greek word in which *hyper* means "beyond" and *bole* means "to throw." *Hyperbole* literally means "a throwing beyond." A *hyperbole* is not a parable because it does not compare situations, but uses obvious exaggeration to make a point.

A simile is figure of speech that shares a resemblance to *parabolē* because it is a comparison of two things using "like" or "as." The Greek language did not have a word for simile, but in many ways *parabolē* is the same thing. In fact, most parables are similes. For the purpose of this book, I have not differentiated between similes and parables; anything that could be called a simile I have categorized as a parable and included.

I believe the other aspect of what separates parables from other types of comparisons is its purpose as a teaching tool. In the case of a *metaphora*, there is not necessarily an aspect of instruction or doctrine (even though there can be), but the comparison is there to relate two things for whatever reason the speaker wants. When a parable is told, especially in the case of Jesus' parables, there is always an element of instruction to the audience that prompted the parable. This seems to be a common understanding of parables outside the ancient Jewish understanding as well.

To summarize, I would say the *sine qua non* of parables, or "without which it is not," is *a comparison of a hypothetical situation to reality emphasizing one similarity to enhance a teaching.* Therefore, a comparison that compares reality to reality, does not have an element of instruction, or uses more than one similarity is not a parable.

Using this definition, we find parables frequently throughout the Gospels. We also find that other qualities of parables, such as the length or whether it is a story or not, do not make the teaching a parable.

We even find the disciples misinterpreting what teachings are a parable. In Matthew 15:11 and Mark 7:15 Jesus says, "Not what goes into the mouth defiles a man; but what comes out of the mouth, this defiles a man." A few verses later, Peter says, "Explain this parable to us" (Matthew 15:15, Mark 7:17). Jesus responds with "Are you still without understanding?" (Matthew 15:16, Mark 7:18). Jesus then proceeds to tell them what He meant: food enters the mouth and is eliminated, but words come out of the heart and defile a man. This explanation does not fit the parable format because Jesus clarifies with more detail what He meant rather than explaining the principle or provoked thought of the comparison. Matthew 15:11 and Mark 7:15 are not comparing a hypothetical situation to reality with one similarity to give a teaching. This is a direct comparison of how eating with unwashed hands does not defile a man but the evil things within his heart expressed in his words do (Matthew 15:20, Mark 7:23). I think Peter heard what sounded like figurative language and mistook it for a parable. Jesus corrected his misunderstanding and clarified what He was saying.

I believe *a comparison of a hypothetical situation to reality emphasizing one similarity to enhance a teaching* is a fair definition of a parable, but I'm not dogmatic about calling a teaching a parable or not. The ultimate point of this study is to gain a better understanding of comparisons Jesus used and apply those teachings to our lives. If there is a comparison that I've missed that you think is a parable or shouldn't be a parable, as long as

9

we are learning rightly dividing that teaching (II Timothy 2:15), calling it a parable or not is a minor issue that should not divide us. In fact, after this book is written I may gain a better understanding of what parables are through the Holy Spirit's guidance and wish I had added or removed comparisons from its contents. Bible study is a life long process, and I hope this book aids in your understanding of Jesus' teachings.

Chapter 3

What is the Purpose of Parables?

Thankfully the Bible tells us exactly what the purpose of parables is in Matthew 13. Jesus tells the parable of the sower, and the disciples ask in 13:10, "Why do you speak to them in parables?" I love it when the Bible defines things for us, much like the Bible defines exactly what we must to do be saved (which is believe) because the Philippian jailer asked the question, "What must I do to be saved?" (Acts 16:30). While Luke and Mark also recount Jesus' answer (Luke 8:9-10, Mark 4:11-12, 4:24-25, 4:33-34), we will focus on Matthew's account because it includes the most detail.

Jesus divides all people into two groups: those that it has been given to know and those to whom it has not been given. Contextually, Jesus is talking about the mysteries of the kingdom parables, but He applies the two groups to all parables in 13:13. He then focuses on the first group: them that it has not been given.

Jesus says of them to whom it has not been given that "whoever does not have, even what he has will be taken away from him" (Matthew 13:11). This is the same phrase used in the parables of the talents and the minas. Jesus is saying that every

11

person has been given an opportunity to understand His message, most importantly that you must believe in Him to have eternal life (John 5:24, Titus 2:11). But they do not understand because "the hearts of this people have grown dull. Their ears are hard of hearing, and their eyes they have closed" (Matthew 13:15, Psalm 78:2). The people did not want to hear or see Jesus' message, so God did not give them the knowledge to understand the parables. Even though they heard the parable, its meaning was concealed from them.

This is much like Pharaoh in the exodus story. Pharaoh rejected the word of God (Exodus 5:2) and therefore God hardened his heart (Exodus 7:3) which caused him to further reject God. In his Epistle, James gives us the same concept when he says "Draw near to God and He will draw near to you" (James 4:8). As we draw near to God we receive more from God, such as grace (James 4:6) and wisdom (James 1:5). However, the opposite is also true that if we don't draw near to God, He will not draw near to us and, for example, we will not receive the wisdom that we could have had. This is what happened to the "it has not been given" group in Matthew 13. They did not draw near to God so He did not give them understanding of the parables.

Jesus also gives the consequence of this lack of understanding. In 13:15 He says, "lest they should see with their eyes and hear with their ears, lest they should understand with their hearts and turn, so that I should heal them." Someone could say at this point, "Why would God keep knowledge from people and not heal them?" The answer lies in the balance of our free will and God control of all things. In order for Jesus to be crucified, He had to be rejected by people who did not understand, or did not want, Him to be the Messiah. God's will was that these people would not be given understanding because if they understood,

He would heal them and Jesus would not have died. However, this does not eradicate their free will because the people had already rejected Jesus as Messiah when they attributed His miracles to Beelzebub (Matthew 12:24). They did not draw near to God, so He did not draw near to them. It is amazing how God is able to keep His will fully intact and also preserve our will to choose!

But does that mean they cannot understand anything that Jesus says in parables? They can understand what God has given them to understand, such as the Pharisees understanding of the parable of the wicked vinedressers (Matthew 21:33-46). Lest anyone think that God was somehow not allowing them to change thier mind and believe, immediately preceding the wicked vinedressers parable was the parable of the two sons, in which Jesus makes it plain that tax collectors and harlots will enter the kingdom of God before the Pharisees because of their belief (Matthew 21:28-32). Hearing these parables incited the Pharisees to devise plots that eventually led to Jesus' death (Matthew 22:15) rather than believe in Him for salvation.

What shall we say to this then? God used parables to both hide and reveal truth to those it had not been given to accomplish His will while never removing their free choice.

Those that is has been given to know, which is the second group, has eyes and ears that are blessed because they see and hear, meaning they understand the parables (Matthew 13:16). In Matthew 13:17, Jesus tells the disciples that many prophets and righteous men desired to see what they are seeing (the coming of the Messiah and His works) and hear what they are hearing (Jesus' sayings).

Jesus says "whoever has, to him more will be given, and he will have abundance" (Matthew 13:12). This is the other half of the phrase that Jesus used to describe those it had not been given and it also appears in the parables of the talents and the minas. The abundance comes from "those that is has been given to know" drawing near to God, God drawing near to them, and giving them more as they draw near.

The second purpose of parables is to fulfill prophecy. Isaiah and Asaph prophesied the Messiah would conceal truth (Isaiah 6:9-10) and reveal truth (Psalm 78:2) in parables.

We can see then in order to be a parable, a teaching must fit both the definition of parable and the purpose of parables by fulfilling prophecy by revealing and concealing truth to the appropriate groups.

There is another aspect about the purpose of parables that isn't directly related to them but rather about how the authors of the Gospels organized their material. The Gospel authors didn't arrange their writings in a strict chronological order. This seems a bit strange to us in modern times because we think any account of historical events should be documented in the order they happened. The Gospel authors did not think this way; they arranged the events of Jesus' life to make a theological point.

For example, all three authors recorded the parable of the sower and the parable of the mustard seed.

In Matthew's Gospel, Jesus tells the multitude the parable of the sower, then the disciples ask Him why He speaks in parables, He gives the explanation of the sower, He tells the parable of the wheat and tares, then He tells the parable of the mustard seed.

In Mark's Gospel, Jesus tells the multitude the parable of the sower, then the disciples ask Him about the parable when Jesus is alone. Jesus tells them the purpose of parables, He gives the explanation of the sower, He tells them the parable of a lamp on a lampstand, He tells the parable of the growing seed, then He tells the parable of the mustard seed.

In Luke's Gospel, Jesus tells the multitude the parable of the sower, then the disciples ask Him why He speaks in parables, He gives the explanation of the sower, but the parable of the mustard seed is not told until a few chapters later.

What is going on? The Gospel writers are not necessarily recording these events in the order they happened. Mark 4:33-34 gives us a further clue:

> And with many such parables He spoke the word to them as they were able to hear it. But without a parable He did not speak to them. And when they were alone, He explained all things to His disciples.
> *Mark 4:33-34*

What this means is the explanation of the parables of the sower and the wheat and tares were not told to the multitudes but only the disciples while they were alone. Matthew puts the explanation of the parable of the sower in his Gospel before Jesus sent the multitudes away (Matthew 13:36), but Mark says this explanation happened while Jesus and His disciples were alone (Mark 4:10). Luke organized the material very differently because he had a different point he was trying to make with his Gospel.

When the Gospels record events such as this in different orders, this is not a reason to doubt the Bible's accuracy or develop theories about how we cannot read the Bible literally. We need to understand that the authors were recording events in the order that made the most sense for whatever theme or theological point they were making.

Matthew organized his material this way because he was

describing the kingdom right after the Jews rejected the offer of the kingdom (Matthew 12:31-32). One of Matthew's main themes is how Jesus is the King even though there is no earthly kingdom present until He returns. Because of this, it made sense to group all of the mystery kingdom parables (except the parable of the growing seed) in one group in the order he wrote them. Mark and Luke had different themes in their writings and organized their material differently.

When we see chronological differences like this, sometimes the parables were told multiple times. Every teacher will end up teaching the same material to different groups at different times and Jesus was no different. For example, Luke records two separate tellings of the parable of a lamp on a lampstand in Luke 8:16 and 11:33. Another example is the parable of the wise and evil servants in Matthew 24:45-51 and Luke 12:42-48. The contexts, audience, and provoked thoughts are different even though the parable is the same. These were two separate occasions where Jesus told the same parable and had a different provoked thought in mind.

Chapter 4

How Parables Should be Explained

All parables share certain characteristics and should be explained using some basic principles.

The first principle of parable interpretation is all parables have a prompt. A prompt can be a question in which the answer is best explained by a parable (ex. parable of the compassionate Samaritan). A prompt can also be a situation (ex. parable of the wedding invitees), an example of a concept being taught (ex. parable of the wise and foolish men), a certain teaching within a discourse (ex. parable of the ten virgins), or an answer to a question posed by the situation (ex. parable of the wicked vinedressers). The prompt can even be something Jesus notices and comments on without the audience first interacting with Him (ex. parable of the praying Pharisee and tax collector). We should always identify the prompt and in doing so it often leads to the correct provoked thought.

Next, all parables have an audience. If Jesus is using a parable, then the audience is relevant to how the parable should be understood. Parables can be taught to a small group such as the disciples (ex. parable of the hidden treasure) or multitudes (ex. parable of the rich fool). When a parable is given to "the

17

multitude," we should generally assume the Pharisees are within the multitude even though we don't know the different classes or occupations which are represented. Whenever the audience includes the disciples, it might be only the twelve but could also include other disciples that followed Jesus. However, in every parable we should assume the audience is Jewish even though Gentiles may be present in a multitude.

All parables have one provoked thought or a central point. Usually this provoked thought is short, but sometimes it is longer and explains different aspects of the same point, such as the parable of the talents in which the provoked thought is about both faithful and unfaithful servants or the parable of the wicked vinedressers which teaches the Jewish leaders' rejection of Jesus and the consequence of that rejection. Different tellings of parables can have different provoked thoughts because of the difference in audience and prompt. There can also be details in the parable that teach truths beyond the provoked thought, such as the parable of the minas. Even though these details are there to teach truths, there is still only one provoked thought or central point to each parable.

The Bible gives us the provoked thought in the majority of parables often signified by Jesus saying "likewise," "so also," "therefore," or a similar phrase. When the Bible gives us the provoked thought, it is usually at the beginning or end of the parable but can also be a repeated phrase within the parable. For parables in which the Bible doesn't give us the provoked thought, we have to interpret it using the context, prompt, and audience to ascertain the meaning.

Parables can often be found in groups, such as the parables of the lost sheep, lost coin, and lost son. Recognizing groupings of similar parables helps to understand the central point because they build upon each other.

Lastly, all parables have details; we must be very careful about assigning meaning to these details. For example, in the parables of the sower and the wheat and tares Jesus assigns meaning to many details because those details are important to understand the provoked thought. Especially in the kingdom parables the details are similar or even exactly what happens in real life, such as how the vinedressers treat the man's servants in the parable of the wicked vinedressers and how Jesus was treated. These details are not the provoked thought but can teach other truths which make the comparison more forceful. Sometimes the details do not have any assignment to the real world, but it is only the situation that has an application to the audience as in the parable of the master and the thief. It is not correct to say the details never have a meaning, but it is also not correct to say every detail always has a meaning.

The meaning of the details of a parable must serve the provoked thought. Most parables have a simple and easy to state provoked thought; if we start assigning meaning to details that detract from this thought or make it more complex than Jesus intended, we are incorrectly interpreting the details of the parable.

By way of example, in the parable of the compassionate Samaritan the provoked thought is to have compassion on your neighbor as the Samaritan had compassion. The detail of the two denarii does not have a meaning other than how much the stay at the inn cost. If we were to say the two denarii equals the two kingdoms of Israel, that would not serve the provoked thought and would even change the central point of the parable. The details of the priest and Levite serve the parable by showing us who did not have compassion and nothing more. While we can gain an application out of this detail that the religious leaders did not show compassion, we wouldn't assign

19

any further or allegorical interpretation to these two story figures.

To state it again, the details of a parable must serve the provoked thought and should not be assigned meaning that does not serve the provoked thought.

Another example is the parable of the mustard seed. The central point of the parable is very simple; the kingdom will start small and grow very large just like a mustard seed is small and grows into a large plant. The details of the parable, the mustard seed being the smallest seed, the plant becoming a tree, and the birds nesting in its branches, are there to emphasize how small the seed is and how large the plant grows. Taking the "birds of the air" as evil being in the kingdom is taking this detail beyond the intent of the parable. While there will be evil in the millennial kingdom, that teaching is not a part of the parable. All the parable is intended to explain is the beginning and ending size of the kingdom.

We must keep the meanings of parables simple; Jesus does this and so should we!

Chapter 5

Background of the Kingdom Parables

Now that we have spent time defining what a parable is and is not, what the purpose of parables are, and how we should interpret them, we are almost ready to begin studying the parables. But before we do, the parables of the kingdom deserve a section to explain their background and how this book understands what the kingdom is.

The kingdom

Jesus tells many parables related to the kingdom, usually started by the phrase, "the kingdom of heaven is like" or a variation. This book takes the position that the "kingdom" is the earthly reign of Christ lasting for 1000 years and continuing for eternity in the eternal state. All of the truths and promises about the kingdom were given to Israel and will be fulfilled through Israel. Furthermore, the Jews viewed the kingdom in the same way we as the Church view heaven: the kingdom/heaven is the final resting place of believers. In this sense, heaven is interchangeable with the use of the word kingdom in the Gospels, even though the first 1000 years of the kingdom/ heaven are on earth.

Whenever Jesus tells parables, the audience is always Jewish and would have understood the definition of the kingdom as an earthly kingdom. The Church did not exist during Jesus' ministry, so the Church cannot be inserted into these parables and there are no parables that directly apply to the Church. It is correct that the Church will be present during the earthly kingdom by Jesus' side (1 Thessalonians 4:17), but that is explained through the Epistles, not in Jesus' ministry.

Some parables talk about what will happen during the tribulation, such as the parable of the ten virgins. Since the Church is not in these parables, the Church must not be on the earth when they take place. Therefore, the rapture must happen before the tribulation occurs.

There are a few parables that talk about a man going away and coming back, such as the parable of the minas in which the man receives a kingdom when he goes away. This means the kingdom is not present now and will not begin until Jesus comes back. This "coming" cannot be the rapture because the rapture is still an unrevealed mystery during Jesus' ministry. There is no other way the kingdom will begin except by Jesus returning to earth at the end of the tribulation.

Even though truths in kingdom parables are not directly applicable to us in the Church, the provoked thoughts can parallel ideas given to the Church. One example is the parable of the master returning from a wedding. The provoked thought is to "be ready, for the Son of Man is coming at an hour you do not expect" (Luke 12:40). While "the coming of the Son of Man" in the parable is Jesus' second coming at the end of the tribulation and not the rapture, Paul tells the Church in 1 Thessalonians 5:6 to "not sleep, as others do, but let us watch and be sober." The Church is supposed to be ready and watch for Jesus' coming at the rapture as the Jews are supposed to watch for Jesus' coming at the end of the tribulation. Therefore, we can still find relevant application in the kingdom parables even though they do not directly apply to us.

I have given a few proofs using the parables to explain how the kingdom parables should be understood, but it is beyond the scope of this book to spend more time explaining the background of Jesus' ministry in relation to the definition and timing of the kingdom. For more information on these topics, I recommend J.B. Hixson's book *What Lies Ahead* and Andy Woods' book *The Coming Kingdom*. Both of these great teachers also have many audio messages about these topics.

Mystery kingdom parables
In Matthew 13, Mark 4, and Luke 8 and 13 there are a series of nine parables that are about "the mysteries of the kingdom of heaven" (Matthew 13:11). The word "mysteries" is translated from the Greek word *mystērion* which means "a secret." *Mystērion* in the Bible carries the meaning of "a secret that is now being revealed." This means the information about the kingdom which is being revealed by these parables was previously unrevealed. Much has been said about what the mysteries are and what the parables mean, and I will do my best to give the correct view on them.

The concepts or ideas in the mystery kingdom parables are not new. For example, the Old Testament reveals a judgment at the end of the age (Ezekiel 20:33-38), not every Jew will enter the kingdom (Zechariah 13:7-9), and there will be Gentiles in the kingdom (Zechariah 14:16-19). If the concepts are not the mystery, then what is it?

I believe the mysteries are the details being revealed about the kingdom, not the concepts themselves. For example, Messiah's kingdom will be a global kingdom (Isaiah 9:7, Daniel 7:14, 7:27) which is also indicated by the parable of the mustard seed

23

(Matthew 13:31). However, the detail the parable reveals is the kingdom will start out small and then grow large. Putting the passages together, Messiah's kingdom will rule over all kingdoms (global), but the beginning of Messiah's kingdom will be small and then grow to a very large kingdom. The small to large size of the kingdom is the mystery being revealed.

More explanation will be given in the chapters about these parables, but I believe the best way to understand the mysteries of the kingdom are the details about the kingdom that are being revealed, not the concepts. Because of this, any explanation of these parables about the Church or faith is misplaced, even though there are applications that parallel the church age and how faith should guide our lives. Any parallels and applications will be explained in the mystery parable chapters.

Outer darkness and weeping and gnashing of teeth
The phrases "outer darkness" and "weeping/wailing and gnashing of teeth" appear in a number of kingdom parables (Matthew 13:42, 13:50, 22:13, 24:51, 25:30, Luke 13:28). The phrases are always used to contrast a person or group that is entering the kingdom to those not entering. Since the kingdom parables are about the Jews and not the Church, these phrases must be dealing with Jews not getting into the kingdom. Outside of parables, "weeping and gnashing of teeth" is used in Matthew 8:12 to tell us very directly that the sons of the kingdom (unbelieving Jews) will not sit down with Abraham, Isaac, and Jacob in the kingdom of heaven but will be cast into outer darkness. They will weep and gnash their teeth because of their extreme regret of missing the kingdom and the torment they will be in.

The term "outer darkness" is used in Matthew 8:12, 22:13, and 25:30 alongside the phrase "weeping and gnashing of teeth." While "weeping and gnashing of teeth" describe what unbelievers will do, outer darkness describes where they will go. Outer darkness is the same as hell just as the kingdom is the same as heaven. Getting sent to outer darkness or hell is conditioned on not believing in the Messiah. Works do not play a part in that destination, and this fact will be elaborated on in the parables that seem to say works are needed to get into the kingdom.

Chapter 6

The Parable of
a Lamp on a Lampstand

Mark 4:21, Luke 8:16 & 11:33

Audience

Multitudes (Mark 4:1, Luke 8:4, 11:29).

Prompt

Jesus told the multitudes four parables about the mysteries of the kingdom as well as this parable. This parable follows the parable of the sower but also could have followed the parable of the wheat and tares which Mark and Luke do not record.

Jesus told this parable again after explaining the Son of Man will be a sign to this generation as Jonah was a sign to the Ninevites (Luke 11:29-32).

Explanation

This parable is told two separate times, once in Mark 4:21 and Luke 8:16 and again in Luke 11:33. The parable is the same both times, but the provoked thought is different. We know this because Jesus gives us the explanation and application in both tellings. The two provoked thoughts of this parable are an explanation of Isaiah 6:9-10 which is quoted by Matthew, Mark, and Luke:

> Keep on hearing, but do not understand;

Keep on seeing but do not perceive,
Make the heart of this people dull,
And their ears heavy,
And shut their eyes:
Lest they see with their eyes,
And hear with their ears,
And understand with their heart,
And return and be healed.
Isaiah 6:9-10

Jesus asks a hypothetical question: is a lightened lamp put under a basket or under a bed? Is it not to be set on a lampstand? Jesus then answers His own question: no one, when he has lit a lamp, covers it with a vessel, puts it under a bed or basket, or puts it in a secret place. They set it on a lampstand that those who enter may see the light.

In the first telling of the parable, Jesus is speaking of revelation that men hear and how it impacts them. Jesus makes the point that God knows people's response to the message of the kingdom and how they will be judged because "there is nothing hidden which will not be revealed, nor has anything been kept secret but that it should come to light" (Mark 4:22). Mark follows this statement in verse 23 with "If anyone has ears to hear, let him hear" which basically means "listen up, this is important!"

Jesus gives a command to be careful about what we hear (Mark 4:24, Luke 8:18) because how we understand and use what we hear will be measured back to us and more will be given based on how much we hear. If we hear something and understand it, God will give us an opportunity to use what we have heard. As we use what we have heard, we will be given more to hear, understand, and use. The more we hear the more we get!

27

But if we hear and do not understand, we will not be given anything. It is our responsibility to understand what Jesus has said because God has given us the ability to understand (Romans 1:20). God has given the message, and we must respond to it, either with understanding or rejection. If we reject the message, which means we do not understand, opportunities to hear will be taken away from us (Mark 4:25, Luke 8:18). This is why Jesus begins with the warning about taking heed to what we hear. We become responsible to use what we hear. If we don't understand and use it even what we have will be consequently taken from us.

If you are reading this, you are now responsible for understanding this teaching. If you use what you have learned from the parables, God will give you more revelation and you will be given more. If you do not use it, God will take away things (who knows what they might be) from you and you will not hear more. The remedy for having things taken away is to confess your sin and God will bring you back into fellowship (1 John 1:9). Only then can we be given more to hear and use.

In the second telling of the parable, Jesus is commenting on the first century Jews being an evil generation and seeking a sign. Jesus likens the lamp in the parable to the eye. Just as a lamp gives light to a room and reveals its contents, the eye gives light to the body and reveals the world to it. The word Jesus used for body is *sōma*. This word doesn't just mean the physical body but the whole person including the soul. What Jesus is saying is your eye reveals things for you to perceive just as a lamp reveals a room for us to perceive what is in it. How we perceive what is revealed will fill our being.

If you are looking at good things and perceiving good out of them, you will be filled with light or good. The disciples (except Judas) saw all the signs they needed in Jesus' miracles to believe in Him. They perceived what they meant, and their body was filled with light. They were seeing and perceiving.

If you are looking at bad things and perceiving evil out of them, you will be filled with darkness or evil. Judas' offer of betrayal was a bad thing and the Pharisees perceived how they could used it for evil. Both were filled with darkness. Judas was so full of darkness he even was filled by Satan (John 13:27).

Beyond seeing good and perceiving good and vice-versa, seeing good and perceiving bad or seeing bad and perceiving good is also possible. Jesus was prompted to tell this parable by the Jews seeking a sign. They already had plenty of signs from Jesus, but they did not perceive them as good. They were still full of darkness even though they saw Jesus' miracles. They were seeing and not perceiving.

On the other hand, Jesus perceived the bad that was in the Pharisees and used that as an opportunity for good to teach the disciples to "beware of the leaven of the Pharisees, which is hypocrisy" (Luke 12:1).

A lamp in a room reveals many things, some good (such as a family picture) and some bad (such as mold). We could perceive those same things differently, hating the picture by being critical of our hair or thinking the mold adds a nice splash of color to the room. Likewise, as our eye reveals the world around us, we can perceive things as good or bad. How we perceive them and what we do with that perception will determine whether our body is filled with light or darkness.

Our eye reveals things for our *sōma* or entire being to perceive and our ear hears things to be understood. If our heart is dull, we will not perceive or understand correctly what we see and hear. May we always be listening to the Holy Spirit's conviction and guiding to be seeing and perceiving as well as hearing and understanding.

Provoked thought

1st telling: Take heed how you hear. For whoever has, to him more will be given; and whoever does not have, even what he seems to have will be taken from him.

2nd telling: Take heed that the light which is in you is not darkness.

Section 1
Mystery Kingdom Parables

Chapter 7

The Parable of the Sower

Matthew 13:3-9 & 18-23, Mark 4:3-8, Luke 8:4-8 & 11-15

Audience

The multitudes were told the parable (Matthew 13:2, Mark 4:1, Luke 8:4) but only the disciples were given the explanation (Matthew 13:18-23, Luke 8:11-15).

Prompt

The multitudes came to Jesus and He told them four parables about the mysteries of the kingdom.

Explanation

A sower went out to sow and his seed fell on different terrain. Some seed fell by the wayside, was trodden, and the birds ate the seed. Some fell on stony places and immediately sprang up because they had no depth of earth; when the sun came up, they withered away because they had no root and lacked moisture. Some fell among thorns and the thorns sprang up with the seeds and choked them. Those yielded no crop. But other seed fell on good ground and yielded a crop; some thirtyfold, some sixty, and some a hundredfold.

After they were alone, Jesus' disciples asked Him why He spoke in parables. After telling them the reason, He explained what the parable of the sower meant. But before we get to the explanation, the question of which of the four types of seed or people are saved always comes up when talking about this parable. We can address this first.

For the seed that fell on the path and was devoured by birds, we can be sure these people are not saved because they do not understand and the word is snatched away (Matthew 13:19, Luke 8:12). In fact, in Luke 8:12 it says clearly, "lest they should believe and be saved."

For the other three seeds, notice in the parable that all three types germinate i.e. the plant starts to grow. The seed on rocky soil sprang up. The seed in the thorns could not be choked by weeds unless there was a plant to choke. And the seeds on the good soil clearly grew into a plant. In Jesus' explanation in Matthew, the word "received" is used of all three seeds in relation to the seed or Word. The Greek word is *spĕirō* which means "to sow." Since the same term is used for all three and we know for sure the seed among good soil believed the Gospel, that must mean all three seeds received the word and believed. But let's continue with a look at the seeds in the rocky and thorny soil.

In Luke's Gospel, the seed among rocky soil is said to believe (Luke 8:13). We can be assured this seed is saved.

Luke 8:14 says the seed among thorns brings no fruit to maturity but hears and goes out. Matthew says they become unfruitful, which means they were fruitful at one time (Matthew 13:22). You cannot be fruitful if you are not saved. We can be assured this seed is saved.

From these evidences we know the seeds in the rocky, thorny, and good soil are all saved, whether they continue in good works or not. Jesus makes it clear that you cannot lose your salvation nor need works to maintain it (John 5:24), but it is beyond the scope of this book to spend time proving the eternal security of the believer. Furthermore, the provoked thought of the parable is not about whether the soils are saved or not, but it is important to note which seeds are believers.

What the provoked thought of the parable is about is how people will react differently to the message of the kingdom.

Some people will reject the message because they do not understand it. Satan has a part in this type of person because we know he is able to blind men's hearts (2 Corinthians 4:4).

Some people will believe the message with joy but will not have a strong foundation. When tribulation or persecution arise because of their faith, they stumble. They go back to an unbelieving lifestyle and do not go on to good works.

Some people will believe the message and do good works for a while. But the cares of this world, how they can make money, and worldly pleasures will influence their thinking. These things will cause them to give up on their good works. They will go back to an unbelieving lifestyle over time and will never reach maturity.

Some people will believe the message and do good works throughout their life. They will not all do the same amount, but they will continue to do them throughout their life with patience.

While all believers struggle to maintain good works throughout their life, we should always have patience in times of doubt. May we have the perseverance to bear fruit in hundredfolds!

Provoked thought

People will react differently to the message of the kingdom. Some will believe and some won't. Some that believe will produce fruit and some won't.

Chapter 8

The Parable of
the Wheat and Tares

Matthew 13:24-30 & 37-43

Audience

The multitudes were told the parable (Matthew 13:2) but only
the disciples were given the explanation (Matthew 13:36).

Prompt

Jesus told the multitudes four parables about the mysteries of
the kingdom. This parable follows the parable of the sower.

Explanation

A man sowed good seed in his field. While he and his servants
slept, his enemy sowed tares in the field. When the grain
sprouted, the servants noticed the tares and asked how the field
had them. The man concluded that an enemy had sowed them.
The servants asked, "Do you want us then to go and gather
them up?" The man replied that he did not want his servants to
gather the tares because they might uproot the grain as well.
Both should grow together until the harvest. When the reapers
harvest the crop, they will separate the tares and wheat in
bundles, burning the tares and putting the wheat in the barn.

Jesus tells this parable to the multitude but privately gives the
explanation to the disciples. The field is the world, the good

seeds are believers, and the tares are unbelievers (Matthew 13:38). The enemy is the devil, the harvest is the end of the age, and the reapers are the angels (Matthew 13:39). The parable is explaining the condition of the world before the kingdom begins.

We don't know exactly what plant the "tares" is, but in some way the servants in the parable were able to distinguish it from the wheat before the harvest. However, if they tried to remove the tares, it would uproot the wheat and kill it. The only way to save the wheat was to wait until harvest time and separate the wheat from the tares after being reaped. Since the wheat and tares are believers and unbelievers respectively that means God will not remove unbelievers until the judgment at the end of the age. They will be together until then, which mean believers will have to deal with the influence that Satan has among them.

But which age and which judgment is it talking about? Jesus uses the term "wailing and gnashing of teeth" in Matthew 13:42. Every other time this phrase is used (Matthew 8:12, 13:42, 13:50, 22:13, 24:51, 25:30, Luke 13:28) it is talking about entrance into the millennial kingdom; it must be talking about it here as well. So the age must be the age of the law which ends at the conclusion the tribulation.

When this judgment happens, the angels will gather all believers and unbelievers. They will cast the unbelievers into the "furnace of fire" or hell where there will be weeping and gnashing of teeth. The righteous will be brought into the kingdom and shine forth as the sun.

This parable is directly applicable to the Jews in the tribulation, but there is a parallel to us in the church age. We will be removed from the world in the rapture instead of unbelievers being removed from our presence, but until then unbelievers are present with us just like this parable. The New Testament is full of warnings to not be influenced or deceived by them (ex. 2 Timothy 3:1-5). We know Satan will also have "tares" that will influence the church (2 Peter 2:1-2). We must be aware that God will not remove them from our midst, but also be on guard against them (Ephesians 6:13-18). So take up the whole armor of God that you may be able to withstand in the evil day!

Provoked thought
Believers and unbelievers will be together until the end of the age of law when they will be separated; believers will enter the kingdom and unbelievers will be cast into hell.

Chapter 9

The Parable of
the Growing Seed

Mark 4:26-29

Audience
Multitudes (Mark 4:1).

Prompt
Jesus told the multitudes four parables about the mysteries of the kingdom. This parable most likely followed the parable of the wheat and tares.

Explanation
A man scattered seed on the ground, went to sleep, and the seed sprouted without him knowing how. The earth yields the crops by itself. When the grain ripens and harvest comes, the man puts the sickle to the grain.

In this kingdom parable, the kingdom is the seed as in the parable of the mustard seed. The seed grows because of the earth and the farmer does nothing to make it grow. The kingdom will grow because of God growing it and man has no part in its growth.

God has been "cultivating" the kingdom since Adam's sin in the garden and Satan became the ruler of earth (Genesis 3:15, Luke 4:6). God's plan for the kingdom "grew" when He made a covenant with Abraham (Genesis 12:1-3, 7, 13:15, 15:1-21). The kingdom did not grow in the sense that the kingdom began and spread on the earth, but its description received more detail through covenants and prophecies in the Old Testament. We are not in the kingdom yet because there has not been a "harvest." God is directing history toward the tribulation and the reign of the Antichrist. At the end of the tribulation, the "grain ripens" and God will "immediately put in the sickle." At that point, the kingdom is ready and God is done "growing" it. The judgment in the parable of the wheat and tares will happen immediately and the kingdom will begin.

As we look at how the kingdom is developed in the Bible, we see that God is responsible for making each major covenant with Israel (Mosiac, Land, Davidic, and New) and giving all prophecy to the prophets. Man has not had any part in this development of what the kingdom will be. As we in the church age draw closer to the rapture, we can see how God is both directing and allowing the world to go into the tribulation. Man may think he is controlling the world, but it is God who has already spoken through the prophets what man will do. From the Fall God has been preparing the world for the kingdom without man's help.

Provoked thought
God is the One preparing the kingdom and man has no part in it's preparation.

Chapter 10

The Parable of
the Mustard Seed

Matthew 13:31-32, Mark 4:30-32, Luke 13:18-19

Audience

In Matthew and Mark, the multitudes came to Jesus (Matthew 13:2, Mark 4:1).

In Luke, the audience is also a multitude but it is possibly a different multitude from the telling of the parable of the sower (Luke 13:17).

Prompt

In Matthew and Mark, Jesus told the multitudes four parables about the mysteries of the kingdom. In Matthew, this parable follows the parable of the wheat and tares. In Mark, it follows the parable of the growing seed.

In Luke, Jesus responds to a ruler of a synagogue, who was angry about Him healing on the Sabbath even though there is nothing wrong with healing on the Sabbath (Luke 13:10-16). Jesus tells this parable after an editorial note by Luke that the religious leaders were put to shame and the multitudes rejoiced over His works (Luke 13:17).

Explanation

The kingdom of heaven is like a mustard seed which is the

smallest of all the seeds. But when it is sown in a field it grows into a large tree and the birds of the air come to nest in it's branches.

The provoked thought of this parable is about the size of the kingdom, starting small and growing very large. It is a very simple point, but the details of the parable have brought it under intense scrutiny. I'm not a botanist, but I will do my best to answer questions about the details of the parable of the mustard seed. We must remember the details will always support the provoked thought. We are going to address common ways the details are interpreted, but we will see the details serve the comparison of a small seed growing into a big plant and should not be taken beyond this point.

There is not unanimous agreement about which mustard plant Jesus is talking about. There are a few accepted possibilities, but each has problems; some don't grow very large or other seeds are smaller. So what is the mustard plant Jesus is talking about? Let's step back a little and remember to whom Jesus is talking.

His audience were Jews who probably knew plenty about farming and plants, but they had not studied and categorized plants in genus, species, etc. like we have in modern times. They knew their plants, but not to the extent modern botanists do. Jesus used the comparison of a mustard seed to the kingdom because it would make sense to them; He was not making a point from a modern botanist's point of view. Furthermore, we do not put the parable of the fig tree under this scrutiny and wonder which kind of fig tree Jesus was talking about.

So which mustard plant is Jesus talking about? After a lot of research, I'm not sure, but that doesn't mean Jesus was wrong or the Bible is inaccurate.

First of all, plants and climates change over time. Humans have

43

been breeding plants for certain qualities for a long time, so plants we see today do not necessarily look like they did 2000 years ago. Not only do plants change, but they may have grown smaller or bigger in a certain area if it had a different climate. This means we can't look at mustard plants today and know exactly how they grew 2000 years ago. Whatever the mustard plant was, it was a small seed that could grow into a large plant. Jesus wouldn't have used this comparison if it wasn't accurate or didn't make sense to His audience.

But someone could say, "But you aren't answering which mustard plant it was." God is not required to preserve the existence of things He talks about in His Word. For example, God describes two animals named Behemoth and Leviathan in Job 40 and 41. There are no living animals in modern times that match these descriptions (at least that we know about). That doesn't mean the animals were not real or the Bible is inaccurate; it only means those animals went extinct. In the same way, God is not required to preserve the exact species of mustard plant that Jesus used as a comparison in this parable. Whatever it was, His audience understood what He meant. According to other ancient Jewish literature, the smallness of the mustard seed was a common comparison for Rabbis around Jesus time, which means Jesus was not the only person to use the comparison.

But someone might also say, "But the mustard seed isn't the smallest seed in the middle east much less the world." Notice in the parable that a sower planted the mustard seed. Of all the seeds that were planted in the Middle East 2000 years ago, the mustard seed is the smallest. So Jesus was accurate is describing the mustard seed as the smallest seed that would be sown.

That same someone (boy, he's got a lot to say!) might point out, "The parable says the mustard seed becomes a tree. Mustard is an herb and herbs aren't trees. This represents the kingdom morphing into something evil." As we explained before, Jesus is not telling the parable from a botanist's point of view. Jesus isn't saying the mustard plant changes into a tree, but the seed grows into something that looks like a tree. Today, there are still mustard plants that look like trees if they are fully grown. His audience would have understood what He meant because they planted mustard seeds and they ended up looking like trees. Jesus wouldn't have used this idea if His audience was unfamiliar with it.

If the mustard seed grows this big, then birds could definitely nest in its branches. Some commentators have said the birds of the air symbolize evil. I don't think this is accurate because that level of detail doesn't serve the provoked thought. The provoked thought is about the kingdom starting very small and growing very large. Including aspects of evil and the kingdom morphing into something evil is beyond the central point of the parable.

By the end of the millennium, the kingdom will cover the four corners of the earth (Revelation 20:8) after starting very small with only the tribulation survivors probably all localized in a small spot on earth (Matthew 24:31). If we also consider the kingdom in the eternal state and we assume the new earth is the same size, the kingdom will grow even larger because there will be no sea in the new earth (Revelation 21:1). Theoretically there will be more room for the kingdom to grow!

Provoked thought
The kingdom will grow to an enormous size compared to its very small beginning size.

Chapter 11

The Parable of the Leaven

Matthew 13:33, Luke 13:20-21

Audience

In Matthew, the multitudes came to Jesus (Matthew 13:2).

In Luke, the audience is also a multitude but it is possibly a different multitude from the telling of the parable of the sower (Luke 13:17).

Prompt

In Matthew, Jesus told the multitudes four parables about the mysteries of the kingdom. This parable follows the parable of the mustard seed.

In Luke, Jesus responds to a ruler of a synagogue, who was angry about Him healing on the Sabbath even though there is nothing wrong with healing on the Sabbath (Luke 13:10-16). Jesus tells this parable after the parable of the mustard seed.

Explanation

The kingdom of heaven can be likened to leaven, which a woman put in three measures of meal until is was all leavened.

In this parable the kingdom of heaven is likened to leaven or yeast. Many explanations of this parable talk about yeast being evil because yeast characterizes evil in other places in Scripture (ex. Luke 12:1). Just because leaven is compared to evil in other passages does not mean it is evil here. In the Old Testament, yeast is not always evil. For example, leaven was not used in bread when the Hebrews left Egypt in Exodus 12:34. Exodus 12:39 tells us the reason they did this was because they were to be driven out so quickly. This had nothing to do with evil but the haste in which they left. Because of this example and a few others, yeast does not always symbolize evil. Furthermore, the leaven is identified as the kingdom of heaven. Yeast can definitely not mean evil in the parable because the kingdom is not evil.

This parable is a further extension of the parables of the growing seed and the mustard seed. The kingdom is being prepared by God in the growing seed and will grow to an enormous size in the mustard seed. This parable explains the kingdom will permeate every part of the world.

Just like the details in the parable of the mustard seed, the detail of the woman hiding the leaven should not be taken further than the central point, such as saying the woman represents evil or the "hiding" represents evil being hidden in the kingdom. This detail explains how leaven is added to dough and how it goes throughout the whole lump. Any assignment of meaning beyond this is going beyond the provoked thought of the parable.

Just as leaven spreads through the entire lump of dough, the kingdom will pervade every part of the world. Yeast even chemically alters the dough; likewise the kingdom will alter life in every part of the world. Jesus will rule with a rod of iron and His justice and righteousness will impact all life everywhere. I don't know about you, but I can't wait for Jesus' rule over the earth and the kingdom to come!

Provoked thought

The kingdom will permeate every part of life in every part of the world.

Chapter 12

The Parable of the Hidden Treasure

Matthew 13:44

Audience
The disciples (Matthew 13:36).

Prompt
Jesus sent the multitudes away and the disciples asked Jesus to explain the parable of the wheat and tares. This parable follows that explanation.

Explanation
The kingdom of heaven is like a treasure hidden in a field, which a man found and hid again. The man sells all that he has and buys the field for the joy of the treasure.

The man in this parable finds a hidden treasure that he wasn't looking for. But when he finds it, it has such great value that is worth more than all his possessions. In the same way, Jesus did not come to earth seeking the Gentiles (Matthew 15:24). Yet there were many Gentiles who believed while He was on earth (Matthew 8:11). Therefore He found them "hidden" within the earth.

The Gentiles who believed while He was on earth, and those after, were of such great value that Jesus died for them. He purchased the "field" or the earth so that any Gentiles could believe and be saved. The kingdom of heaven will include the "treasure" that Jesus now owns: the Gentiles. How thankful are we Gentiles that Jesus found us so valuable that He died for us and not just God's chosen nation of Israel!

Provoked thought

Jesus paid the purchase price for any Gentile to enter the kingdom of heaven.

Chapter 13

The Parable of
the Pearl of Great Price

Matthew 13:45-46

Audience
The disciples (Matthew 13:36).

Prompt
Jesus sent the multitudes away and the disciples asked Jesus to explain the parable of the wheat and tares. This parable follows the parable of the hidden treasure.

Explanation
The kingdom of heaven is like merchant seeking beautiful pearls. When he found one pearl of great price, he sold all that he had and bought it.

This parable likens the kingdom of heaven to a merchant seeking pearls. The merchant must be Jesus, who came to seek and save the lost (Luke 19:10). Salvation is available to everyone, but Jesus was sent specifically to the house of Israel (Matthew 15:24). Therefore Israel must be the "pearl."

Just like the man in the parable of the hidden treasure, the merchant in this parable sells all that he has to own the pearl. Jesus purchased Israel with His own blood so they could believe and be saved. Not that all Israel will be saved, but just like the

Gentiles, they all have the opportunity to be saved because of Jesus' payment. How wonderful that Jesus, even though they rejected Him at His first coming, found Israel so valuable that He died for them so that they could enter their kingdom!

Provoked thought

Jesus paid the purchase price for Israel to enter the kingdom of heaven.

Chapter 14

The Parable of the Dragnet

Matthew 13:47-50

Audience

The disciples (Matthew 13:36).

Prompt

Jesus sent the multitudes away and the disciples asked Jesus to explain the parable of the wheat and tares. This parable follows the parable of the pearl of great price.

Explanation

The kingdom of heaven is like a dragnet that was cast into the sea and gathered some of every kind of fish. The fisherman drew in the net when it was full and separated the good fish from the bad fish. The good were gathered into vessels and the bad were thrown back into the sea.

From the parables of the hidden treasure and the pearl of great price, we know all Gentiles and Jews have the opportunity to enter the kingdom of heaven because Jesus purchased them with His blood. This parable explains that not everyone who has the opportunity to enter the kingdom will get in.

The fishing net caught some fish of every kind. At the end of the tribulation, some of every nation that is left will be gathered by the angels before Jesus. The angels will separate the wicked from the just (Matthew 13:49). This is the same judgment as the harvest in the parable of the wheat and tares. Jesus' explanation of this parable does not say it, but we know from other Scriptures that what makes people just or wicked is whether they believed in Jesus as Savior (Matthew 8:10-12). The wicked will be cast into the furnace of fire or hell where there will be wailing and gnashing of teeth (Matthew 13:50).

Since Jesus does not mention the righteous entering into the kingdom of heaven, the emphasis is on those who will not enter the kingdom. Everyone is "caught in the net" or brought before Jesus and examined. Everyone has the opportunity to enter the kingdom based on their response to the Gospel, but those who do not believe will not enter the kingdom.

Reader, do you believe in Jesus who died for your sins and rose from the grave? He purchased you and all you must do is believe that message and you will be one of the "good fish" that enters heaven. I pray that you do!

Provoked thought
All peoples will be gathered before Jesus at the end of the tribulation; the wicked will be separated from the just and thrown into hell.

Chapter 15

The Parable of the Householder

Matthew 13:52

Audience
The disciples (Matthew 13:36).

Prompt
Jesus sent the multitudes away and the disciples asked Jesus to explain the parable of the wheat and tares. After telling the disciples the parable of the dragnet, He asks His disciples if they understood all that He told them (Matthew 13:51). This parable follows their response that they understood.

Explanation
The kingdom of heaven is like a householder who brings out of his treasure new and old things.

Jesus likens every scribe instructed concerning the kingdom to a householder. The householder's treasures are not only old things but also new. The disciples have just been given a wealth of new information about the kingdom through the preceding eight parables. The new information compliments all the old information about the kingdom that is contained in the Old Testament. They are to put all of this knowledge together for a more complete description of the kingdom.

Just like the householder's treasure is both new and old, the new information about the kingdom contained in these eight parables is not more valuable than information in the Old Testament or vice-versa. All of it creates a complete picture of the kingdom. In fact, new information about the kingdom will still be added in the book of Revelation, such as the length of the earthly millennial kingdom (Revelation 20:4).

Now that the canon of Scripture is complete (Jude 3), we have all the information about the kingdom God revealed. When we study the kingdom, we must put together all the information about the kingdom before Christ's first coming, during, and after to have a complete picture.

Provoked thought
To understand the kingdom, both new and old information must be put together.

Section 2

Kingdom Parables

Chapter 16

The Parable of
the Friends of the Bridegroom

Matthew 9:15, Mark 2:19-20, Luke 5:34-35

Audience

This parable is told either while Jesus was dining at Levi's (Matthew) house or after. In Luke's Gospel it sounds as if the Pharisees ask Him about fasting immediately after Jesus' answer to why He was eating and drinking with tax collectors and sinners. In Matthew and Mark's Gospels it sounds as if this parable happened after the dinner, possibly because they noticed He was eating while they were fasting. It is also possible that the disciples of John in Matthew's Gospel asked Jesus about fasting apart from when the Pharisees asked about the subject in Luke. In Mark it sounds as if they are all together. Whether or not the Gospels are recounting different events with the same parable or the same event, we know that John's disciples, the Pharisees, and Jesus' disciples were present. It is also possible that Levi and his guests were in the audience.

Prompt

The Pharisees and the disciples of John were fasting and asked why Jesus' disciples were not fasting.

Explanation

Jesus answers the question of why His disciples are not fasting with a comparison to a Jewish wedding ceremony. Jesus is referring to the part of the wedding in which the bridegroom's friends are with him, and they are going to retrieve the bride to begin the final part of the ceremony (the entire ceremony lasted about a year). This is obviously a joyous time for the bride and bridegroom because they will soon be married! But, Jesus says, there will come a day when the bridegroom will be taken away and then there will be mourning.

Even though a time of fasting can be a joyous occasion (Zechariah 8:19), in general fasting was a time of mourning throughout the Old Testament. The Old Testament talks about fasting as mourning as:

- Part of the Day of Atonement
    Leviticus 16:29-34
- Part of supplication for national sins
    1 Samuel 7:5-6, Ezra 8:21, Jeremiah 14:11-12, Daniel 9:3-4, Joel 2:12
- Part of supplication for personal sins
    2 Samuel 20:22-23

Jesus also assumes fasting is a time of mourning, which prompts the comparison between when joy should and should not happen during a wedding ceremony. Jesus, the bridegroom, is here and His friends, the disciples, should rejoice as the friends of a bridegroom rejoice during the ceremony. But if the bridegroom is not present, as Jesus will eventually not be present after His ascension, it is not a time of joy any more; fasting will be appropriate. The answer to the Pharisees and John's disciples is one of timing, that mourning and thus fasting are not appropriate while Jesus is present.

Provoked thought
Since Jesus is present, it is a time of joy and not mourning.

Chapter 17

The Parable of
the New Cloth and Old Garment

Matthew 9:16, Mark 2:21, Luke 5:36

Audience
John's disciples, the Pharisees, Jesus' disciples, and possibly Levi's (Matthew) dinner guests (see the audience of the parable of the friends of the bridegroom for a complete explanation).

Prompt
This parable follows the parable of the friends of the bridegroom after the Pharisees and the disciples of John asked why Jesus' disciples do not fast.

Explanation
This parable builds on the previous parable, the friends of the bridegroom. Jesus explains that no one repairs an old or used garment with a new piece of cloth or a cloth from a new garment. If someone were to do that, the patched piece of cloth would tear the old garment when it gets wet or because it is not done stretching or "settling in." This makes a new tear or makes the original tear worse. Furthermore, the new piece of cloth will never match the old garment because the old garment is worn and distressed.

Much like the friends of the bridegroom, Jesus is comparing

what is appropriate while He is present to when He is not present. While fasting is appropriate in anticipation of the Messiah, fasting and mourning are not appropriate while He is here. You would not be joyful during a time of morning or else the mourning is made worse. When this happens, the person who is joyful at a time of mourning is not appreciated and often times the mourners are made angry by his joy which increases their sorrow. The joyful person is "tearing the old garment."

If John's disciples and the Pharisees understood the times, they would understand their fasting is incompatible with Jesus' presence. If the joy of the Messiah's presence was happening during the waiting and mourning period for the Messiah, the mourning is made greater because the mourners now have to deal with someone who misunderstands the times. As Ecclesiastes 3:4-5 says, "A time to weep, and a time to laugh; a time to mourn and a time to dance."

Provoked thought
The joy that represents the Messiah's presence is incompatible with the mourning that represents the awaiting of His arrival.

Chapter 18

The Parable of
New and Old Wine and Wineskins

Matthew 9:17, Mark 2:22, Luke 5:37-38

Audience

John's disciples, the Pharisees, Jesus' disciples, and possibly Levi's (Matthew) dinner guests (see the audience of the parable of the friends of the bridegroom for a complete explanation).

Prompt

This parable follows the parable of the new cloth and old garment after the Pharisees and the disciples of John asked why Jesus' disciples do not fast.

Explanation

Jesus tells a third parable to explain the question of why His disciples are not fasting. He says no one puts new wine into old wineskins because the wineskin will burst. The wine is spilled and the wineskin is ruined. New wine must be put into new wineskins which preserves both of them.

When Jesus talks about new wine, He is assuming the fermentation process has not completed or possibly even started. It was the custom of the day to put wine into wineskins made of goat skin. Over time, a wineskin would become old and weaken. During fermentation, gas is released which expands the wineskin, and if the wine was placed in an old wineskin, which could not resist the expanding gas, it would burst.

Another possibility for why Jesus says the wineskin will burst is the winemaker wants to preserve the wine in the same state as when he put it in the wineskin. If he used the old wineskin, there would be yeast, the fermentation agent, still residing inside the wineskin. When the new wine comes in contact with the yeast, air is introduced into the skin and fermentation would begin. If this is the situation Jesus is talking about, the old wineskin would burst not necessarily from being old, but because the residual yeast causes fermentation and the expanding gas would cause any wineskin to break. Either way, you do not put new wine into old wineskins.

Now that Jesus is here, He is fulfilling the Law and the Prophets (Matthew 5:17). Once the kingdom begins, behaviors will change because Jesus is ruling and there is peace (Isaiah 9:7). For example, during the kingdom a child could play by a snake den and not get hurt (Isaiah 11:8-9). If a child did that in the current time, I don't think there would be the same result and "the wineskin would burst!"

Like the previous parable, Jesus is contrasting what is appropriate while the King is present to what is appropriate while the King is absent. The joy of the kingdom would "tear," "not match," and "burst" during the time of anticipation for the kingdom. If you tried to act like we are in the kingdom now, at best your efforts are wasted (wine is spilled) and at worst it would be harmful (playing by a snake's den). But if kingdom behaviors are performed during the kingdom and non-kingdom behaviors are done before the kingdom, the effectiveness or "wine" is preserved.

Provoked thought
Kingdom behaviors would be wasted before the kingdom appears.

Chapter 19

The Parable of Old Wine

Luke 5:39

Audience
John's disciples, the Pharisees, Jesus' disciples and possibly Levi's (Matthew) dinner guests (see the audience of the parable of the friends of the bridegroom for a complete explanation).

Prompt
This parable follows the parable of the new and old wine and wineskins after the Pharisees and the disciples of John asked why Jesus' disciples do not fast.

Explanation
Jesus tells a parable that no one immediately desires new wine after drinking old wine for old wine is better.

Over time, the aging process of wine will change the flavor because of the reactions between the sugar, acids, and other substances in the wine. These reactions give the wine a more pleasing flavor and can even change the color, aroma, and texture. Jesus is comparing the better "old wine" of the kingdom to the "new wine" before the kingdom.

Once someone "drinks old wine" or experiences kingdom conditions, they would not desire the pre-kingdom state or the "new wine." For instance, the beatitudes satisfy all of the deficiencies of the present world (Luke 6:20-23). Once you have "tasted" these things and have been satisfied, you would not want to go back to being hungry, weeping, etc. Jesus is offering a better "wine" or time of joy rather than a time of mourning and "new wine."

Jesus is not saying the kingdom is present, but that the King is on earth and His disciples are acting appropriately in His presence. After Jesus ascends, His disciples will change their behavior again to anticipate the kingdom and the King's arrival. They will fast in those days because fasting will be appropriate. Yet we will still be able to rejoice in the Lord (Philippians 4:4)!

Instead of plainly stating "My disciples don't fast because now is not the time," Jesus gives us such a vivid picture of why they are not fasting. I pray this group of parables excite you for the kingdom and encourage you to have the proper attitude while awaiting it!

Provoked thought
Kingdom conditions are better than pre-kingdom conditions.

Chapter 20

The Parable of
a Kingdom Divided

Matthew 12:25, Mark 3:24-25, Luke 11:17

Audience

The multitudes (Matthew 12:23, Mark 3:20, Luke 11:14).

Prompt

Jesus just finished casting out a demon that caused a man to be mute and blind. The multitudes were amazed and asked themselves, "Could this be the Son of David?" The Pharisees did not want Jesus to be the Messiah and accused Jesus of casting out the demon by Beelzebub, the ruler of demons (Matthew 12:22-24). This parable is preceded by Jesus saying, "How can Satan cast out Satan?" (Mark 3:23).

Explanation

Jesus explains no kingdom, house or city divided against itself can stand. It will fall.

This was not the first time Jesus had cast out demons (Mark 3:11), so it was clear by this exorcism that Satan's kingdom was still present. Jesus is explaining that if He was doing as the Pharisee's suggested, Satan's rule of his kingdom (the earth) would end because rebellion would be within his ranks. If the Pharisees were right, Jesus, as Satan's subordinate, would be using Satan's name to dethrone him as king. Satan's kingdom would be divided and would fall if Jesus were a part of his kingdom. This parable is demonstrating that Jesus is clearly not part of Satan's kingdom and Satan still has rule over his kingdom because of the continued demonic activity.

Then Jesus suggests that if He casts out demons by the Spirit of God, the kingdom of God has come upon them, meaning the King is here to bring in His kingdom. He also asks by who's authority other Jews cast out demons (Luke 11:19). Those who cast out demons by God's authority will judge the Pharisees because the Pharisees accused Jesus of casting them by by Beelzebub.

Provoked thought
Jesus cannot be casting out demons by Satan because that would render an end to Satan's kingdom.

Chapter 21

The Parable of
the Strong Man

Matthew 12:29, Mark 3:27, Luke 11:21-22

Audience
The multitudes (Matthew 12:23, Mark 3:20, Luke 11:14).

Prompt
Jesus told this parable after the parable of a kingdom divided which was prompted by the Pharisees accusing Jesus of casting out demons by Beelzebub.

Explanation
A fully armed strong man guards his palace, protecting his goods and keeping everyone out. The strong man trusts in his defenses against anyone who would want to take his goods.

Building off what He explained in the parable of a kingdom divided, Jesus further explains what He is doing to Satan's kingdom. When a man who is stronger than the strong man comes, the stronger man is able to overpower the other man and bind him. After the strong man has been bound, the stronger plunders all the armor and goods which the strong man trusted in.

In this parable, Jesus is the stronger man who is plundering the strong man's house, which is Satan's house or kingdom. Satan apparently believes his defenses are still strong enough to withstand God's power. Satan believed he could be like God (Isaiah 14:13-14) when he fell, and I believe Jesus is saying he still has the same attitude. Even in Revelation we see Satan still trying to ascend above God's kingdom (Revelation 20:7-9). We can deduce from this that Satan is so warped in his thinking that nothing can dissuade him from believing he can be like God.

From this parable we receive instruction about how we are to view and interact with Satan even though Jesus directed this parable to the first century Jews. If Satan is the strong man, only a stronger man can plunder his house. We are not the strong man but Jesus is. Therefore, Jesus is the only one capable of advancing against Satan's kingdom. We should not try to destroy Satan's kingdom; we are to stand our ground, resisting Satan until Jesus returns to bind him (James 4:7, 1 Peter 5:9, Ephesians 6:11-13).

Jesus concludes the parable with the statement, "He who is not with Me is against Me, and he who does not gather with Me scatters" (Luke 11:23). There is no middle ground between Satan's kingdom and God's kingdom. Either you are with the strong man or you are with the stronger man who will plunder him.

The Pharisees aligned with Satan's kingdom by attributing Jesus' miracles to Beelzebub. This caused Jesus to withdraw the offer of the kingdom to the first century Jews, a decision that could not be reversed (Matthew 12:31-32). If they would have followed the conviction of the Holy Spirit (John 16:8-9) and believed in Jesus as the Messiah, they would have aligned themselves with the kingdom of God and the kingdom would have begun. Their disbelief is what caused this "unpardonable sin."

The same can be said for our souls. Every sin we commit will be forgiven except the sin of unbelief. This sin will send us to hell for eternity where we will be separated from God and tormented. Reader, I pray you have trusted in Jesus as your Savior Who died for your sins on the cross, Who gives you eternal life to be in heaven with Him. Once you have believed in Him, I pray you will stand against Satan who will one day be defeated.

Provoked thought

Jesus will plunder Satan's kingdom when the kingdom of God appears.

Chapter 22

The Parable of the Great Supper

Luke 14:16-24

Audience
Invitees at the house of one of the rulers of the Pharisees (Luke 14:1).

Prompt
After telling the parables of the dinner invitees and the dinner host, a man at the table said to Jesus, "Blessed is he who shall eat bread in the kingdom of God!" (Luke 14:15).

Explanation
A man planned a great supper and invited many. When the supper was ready, he sent his servant to announce to the invited that the supper was ready. But the invited all made excuses, such as business deals and marriage, to be excused from the supper. The servant reported their responses to his master. The master was angry and instructed the servant to invite the poor, maimed, lame, and blind. However, after inviting them there was still room. The master again instructed the servant to go out into the highways and hedges and compel those he found to come so that his house may be filled. The master also rejected those he originally invited from having any part in the supper.

The man who said, "Blessed is he who shall eat bread in the kingdom of God!" probably did not understand or at least did not care about the message of humbleness Jesus was trying to get across to those at the table. It seems he is assuming those invited by the Pharisee, presumably Pharisees themselves, would get into the kingdom. While at the house of the Pharisee they were watching Jesus closely (Luke 14:1), most likely to accuse Him of something because by this time Jesus had made enemies with the Pharisees (ex. Luke 13:10-17). Their intentions for inviting Jesus were not pure, which means the assumption that they will enter the kingdom is very out of place.

Jesus used this parable to explain who will get into kingdom. The Jews are the ones who are "invited" to be a part of the kingdom. Jesus' ministry was telling them the "supper is ready." He said "the kingdom of heaven is at hand" (Matthew 4:17). But the Jews made excuses when presented with clear evidence that Jesus was the Messiah, saying "this fellow does not cast out demons except by Beelzebub, the ruler of demons" (Matthew 12:24). Jesus then took away the offer of the kingdom (Matthew 12:31-32), which meant those that were invited were no longer welcome.

Jesus no longer presented Himself to the religious leaders as their Savior, but instead began a more private ministry to "the poor and the maimed and the lame and the blind." These are the "uninvited," the ones who did not have the ability to crown Jesus as King of Israel because they were not the leaders of the nation. Nevertheless, they believed in Him, and thus were welcomed into the "supper" or the kingdom of heaven. Yet God's plan for who is in the kingdom does not stop there.

The next people that will get into the kingdom are those on "the highways and hedges" or the Gentiles. This is a prediction of the Church age, of Jews and Gentiles in one body as part of the kingdom. Notice the parable ends before the supper begins. That means that while those on the highways and hedges (the Gentiles) are being invited, the supper (the kingdom) has not begun. The kingdom will only begin when Jesus returns, which is made clear in other parables.

The Pharisees did not understand that entrance into the kingdom starts with humbleness, a humbleness that understands the righteousness heaven demands is perfect righteousness (Matthew 5:38) and the only way to get that righteousness is to believe in Jesus (John 3:16, Genesis 15:6). I pray that you, reader, are humble and do not make excuses when invited to the supper.

Provoked thought
None of those men who were invited (Jewish religious leaders) shall taste God's supper (entrance into the kingdom).

Chapter 23

The Parable of
the Persistent Widow

Luke 18:1-8

Audience
Jesus is speaking to the disciples (Luke 17:22), but the Pharisees may have heard too (Luke 17:20).

Prompt
Jesus spoke this parable after His description of what will happen at the end of the tribulation (Luke 17:22-37) to explain that men always ought to pray and not lose heart (Luke 18:1).

Explanation
A widow came to a judge who did not fear God nor regard man and said, "Get justice for me from my adversary." The widow kept coming to judge even though he would not make a ruling. After awhile the judge said to himself, "Though I do not fear God nor regard man, yet because this widow troubles me I will avenge her, lest by her continual coming she weary me."

Jesus gives us His own commentary on this parable as soon as He finishes telling it. He tells us to focus on what the unjust judge said: "Though, I do not fear God nor regard man, yet because this widow troubles me I will avenge her, lest by her continual coming she weary me" (Luke 18:4-5). Jesus then relates God to the judge by saying, "Shall God not avenge His own elect who cry out day and night to Him, though He bears long with them?" (Luke 18:7). Jesus is saying that even though God does not avenge us right away, He will avenge those who are persistent in crying out to Him. When God does avenge us, the justice will come speedily as the next verse says. Nevertheless, Jesus says, will the Son of Man find faith on the earth when He comes?

God will avenge His own elect (believers) quickly when the Son of Man comes the second time at the end of the tribulation. By the question of finding faith when Jesus does come, He may be indicating the number of believers at the end of the tribulation will be small. He could also be saying that of the believers that are left, will they have lost heart and not be praying for God to avenge them?

This parable is encouraging the generation of believers in the tribulation, and by extension all of us, to always pray and not lose heart because God will eventually bring justice to the earth when Jesus returns. For us in the Church age, we should not avenge ourselves but give place for wrath for vengeance is the Lord's and He will repay (Romans 12:19, Deuteronomy 32:35). So until we come back with Him,

> If your enemy is hungry, feed him; if he is thirsty, give him a drink; for in so doing you will heap coals of fire on his head. Do not be overcome with evil, but overcome evil with good.
> *Romans 12:20-21*

Provoked thought
Men always ought to pray and not lose heart.

Chapter 24

The Parable of
the Unforgiving Servant
Matthew 18:23-35

Audience
The disciples (Matthew 18:1).

Prompt
Peter asked Jesus how many times he should forgive his brother
if his brother kept sinning against him (Matthew 18:21).

Explanation
The kingdom of heaven is like a king who wanted to settle
accounts with his servants. A servant who owed ten thousand
talents was not able to pay, so the king commanded his family
and all his possessions be sold. The servant begged the master
to have patience so he could pay the debt. The king had
compassion, released him, and forgave the debt. But the servant
found a fellow servant who owed him one hundred denarii and
demanded that he pay the debt after choking him. The fellow
servant begged him to have patience so he could pay the debt.
But the servant would not, and threw the fellow servant in
prison until he paid the debt. Other servants told the king what
happened. The king called the servant and said, "You wicked
servant! I forgave you all your debt because you begged me.
Should you not also have had compassion on your fellow

servant, just as I had pity on you?" The king was angry and delivered the servant to the torturers until he paid his debt.

Even though this parable sounds like it is about getting into the kingdom because God forgives us of our sin when we believe, it is about sanctification among believers. We are not denied entrance to or removed from the kingdom because we do not forgive others. But if we do not forgive others, there are consequences for our lack of forgiveness.

The servant owed a lot of money to his master, possibly close to 60 million dollars in today's money. But because he begged his master for time to pay, his master forgave all his debt. No matter how many sins we have committed, God always forgives all of them completely because "where sin abounded, grace abounded all the more" (Romans 5:20). He is faithful and just to forgive us and cleanse us from unrighteousness (I John 1:9). In the kingdom, Jesus will show great compassion for all people and forgive any sin they commit except unbelief (John 16:9).

The servant did not show this same attitude to his fellow servant. The fellow servant owed him far less money, about 11 to 12 thousand dollars in today's money. He begged for time to repay the debt, but the owed servant showed no compassion. When the master learned of the servant's actions, he un-forgave the debt and had the servant delivered to torturers until the debt was paid. During the kingdom, Jesus will show great compassion but He will also rule with a rod of iron and deal justice to those who sin (ex. Zechariah 14:16-19).

In the same way, if we do not show the same compassion and forgiveness to our brethren as God has shown us, we will pay the consequences for our sin of unforgiveness. We must forgive from our heart (not just saying the words) the trespasses of others as Jesus told us to do in the Lord's prayer, more correctly named the disciple's prayer (Matthew 6:12). Paul echos this in Ephesians 4:32 by writing, "be kind to one another, tenderhearted, forgiving one another, even as God in Christ forgave you."

Provoked thought
God will make us pay the consequences of our sin, if each of us, from our heart, does not forgive his brother.

Chapter 25

The Parable of the Vineyard Workers

Matthew 20:1-16

Audience
The disciples (Matthew 19:23).

Prompt
Peter asked what the disciples should receive for leaving all and following Jesus. This parable follows Jesus' statement, "many who are first will be last, and the last first" (Matthew 19:30).

Explanation
The kingdom of heaven is like a landowner who went out early in the morning to hire laborers for his vineyard. He found laborers, agreed on a denarius for the work, and sent them to the vineyard. He went to the marketplace about the third hour and hired those who were idle, saying he would pay whatever is right. He did this again at the sixth and ninth hours. About the eleventh hour he went out again and found those that no one hired and sent them to the vineyard promising to pay whatever was right. When evening came, all the laborers were called to receive their wages. Those that were hired at the eleventh hour were given a denarius as well as the first laborers. Those that were hired first complained because they were made equal with those who worked one hour. The landowner replied that he did

no wrong because they agreed on a denarius for payment. He wished to pay the last men the same as the first and it is lawful for him to do what he wants with his own money. He concluded by asking if the first hires had an evil or greedy eye because of his goodness to all the workers.

In the kingdom, those who labored during their earthly lives will receive rewards. But God will not give out rewards in the way we might expect. The laborers in the parable who were hired first worked all day but received the same wage as those who only worked one hour (the landowner would have hired the first about six o'clock in the morning and the eleventh hour is five o'clock in the afternoon). Likewise, those who were saved for most of their earthly lives may receive the same reward as one who worked a much shorter time. In this, the first will be last and the last first.

We could speculate why those who are able to work longer receive the same wage as those who work shorter, but we know that God will be fair because He renders "to each one according to his work" (Psalm 62:12). Any works not built on the foundation of Christ will be burned (I Corinthians 3:12-15). Even though these verses are about the Church, it seems the same principle of work being burned if not built on God's foundation will apply to Israel.

In this way, those we think will earn many rewards will not necessarily earn many. My opinion is that we will be very surprised about who receives the most rewards. There may be those who spent many hours privately praying instead of works which are seen. The first we think of to receive a large wage may be the last in terms of how much they receive.

All believers of all ages are called to work for God (Matthew 20:16). We are all given opportunities to work, whether it is evangelizing in public or praying privately. When Jesus says "but few chosen" in Matthew 20:16 I believe He is referring to those who are chosen by God to earn large wages. There have been many believers throughout history, and many will be unproductive as the parable of the sower points out. The New Testament exhorts believers to be productive often. For example the apostle John instructs believers to abide in Christ, "that when He appears, we may have confidence and not be ashamed before Him at His coming" (I John 2:28). The entire book of Hebrews is exhorting believers to stay productive and continue in the faith.

One motivation for carrying on in faith is to earn rewards. This is not a selfish or greedy desire, but one that aligns with our new man to serve and glorify God (Colossians 2:10). Paul at the end of his life was looking forward to the crown he would be given at the judgment seat of Christ (II Timothy 4:8). After we are given our rewards, we will lay them down at the feet of Jesus (Revelation 4:10) because we recognize it was Him who gave us the ability to earn them in the first place. It is a perfect picture of God rewarding faithful service and us recognizing Who's glory the rewards were for.

Provoked thought
The last will be first, and the first last. For many are called, but few chosen.

Chapter 26

The Parable of
the Two Sons

Matthew 21:28-32

Audience

The chief priests, elders, Pharisees, and anyone else in the temple (Matthew 21:23, 21:45-46).

Prompt

The chief priests and the elders of the people questioned Jesus' authority (Matthew 21:23). Jesus would not tell them where His authority came from because they did not answer whether the baptism of John was from God or man.

Explanation

There was a man who asked his two sons to work in his vineyard. The first said he would not go, but regretted not going and went to work. The second said he would go but did not. Jesus asked the chief priests and elders which did the will of his father. They correctly answered the first son.

Jesus was putting the chief priests and elders in a tough position from their standpoint. By this time, they knew where Jesus' authority came from (John 8:14-19). Among other reasons, Jesus threatened their position and power so they sought to put Him to death (John 11:45-48). When they were asking Him about His authority in our passage, they were not asking to learn the answer. They were asking Jesus to entangle Him in His talk the same way they would do later (Matthew 22:15).

Jesus asked whether John's baptism was from God or man. No matter how they answered, they would do damage to themselves. They didn't answer the question, so Jesus didn't tell them where His authority came from (even though they knew). Jesus tells this parable to make clear that it is better to change your mind when you are wrong than to continue being wrong.

Jesus uses the parable in the form of a question to His audience and He explains exactly what He meant by the teaching that the chief priests and elders need to change their mind like the first son. John's baptism came in the way of righteousness and the chief priests and elders did not believe him. However, the tax collectors and harlots did believe him. Instead of seeing the effect John's ministry was having on people and regretting their decision to not believe his message, the chief priests and elders still did not believe him. Because of this, the tax collectors and harlots, who the religious leaders looked down upon, will enter the kingdom of God before the chief priests and elders because they will not enter it at all.

Jesus is pointing out the chief priests and elders are like the second son. They say they follow God but do not believe His messengers, even Jesus. Instead the religious leaders should be like the first son that did not do his father's will, but afterward regretted it and did.

If you have never placed your faith in Jesus, now is the time to change your mind and believe that He died for your sins. Do not be like the first century Jews, who had every sign available to prove Who Jesus was but never changed their mind and believed.

If you have placed your faith in Christ, if you are making decisions against His will, now is the time to regret your decisions and do His will. He will not chide you for your past, but will forgive you and give you freely what you ask in faith (1 John 1:9, James 1:5).

Provoked thought
Better to change your mind and do the will of the God than say you are doing His will and not do it.

Chapter 27

The Parable of
the Wicked Vinedressers

Matthew 21:33-44, Mark 12:1-12, Luke 20:9-16

Audience
Chief priests, elders, Pharisees, anyone else in the temple (Matthew 21:23, 21:45-46).

Prompt
This parable immediately follows the parable of the two sons after the chief priests and elders of the people questioned Jesus' authority (Matthew 21:23). Jesus would not tell them where His authority came from because they did not answer whether the baptism of John was from God or man.

Explanation
Knowing the religious leaders would not change their mind and believe in Him, Jesus tells another parable to explain why the kingdom will be taken from them.

A man planted a vineyard with a hedge, a winepress, and a tower. He left the vineyard for a far away country after leasing it to vinedressers. When vintage-time came, the owner sent his servants to receive the fruit, but the vinedressers wounded, beat, stoned, and killed them. Lastly he sent his son, thinking they would respect him. The vinedressers plotted to kill him to gain his inheritance and did so. Jesus asked the religious leaders, "When the owner of the vineyard comes, what will he do to those vinedressers?" They answered the owner "will destroy the wicked men miserably, and lease his vineyard to other vinedressers who will render to him the fruits in their seasons." Jesus repeated their response to confirm their answer was correct. Others answered "Certainly not!" for maybe they thought the treatment was too harsh.

As in the parable of the two sons, Jesus tells us exactly what the parable means. He quotes Psalm 119:22-23, which says, "The stone which the builders rejected has become the chief cornerstone. This was the LORD's doing and it is marvelous in our eyes." Jesus is the chief cornerstone and the religious leaders are the builders who rejected Him.

In the parable, the religious leaders are the vinedressers who killed the servants and the man's son. Likewise, the religious leaders killed God's servants, the prophets, and God's son. The kingdom was offered to Israel in Jesus' first coming, but they rejected Him. The offer was taken away just as the kingdom was taken from them. They will be destroyed just as the vinedressers were destroyed.

But at the end of the tribulation, the tribulation generation of Jews will accept Jesus as their King. That nation, the generation of believing Jews, will bear the fruits of the kingdom and they will receive the kingdom.

Jesus says, "whoever falls on this stone will be broken; but on whomever it falls, it will grind him to powder" (Matthew 21:44, Luke 20:18). This means whoever does not believe in Jesus, or falls on this Stone, will be broken, or not enter the kingdom. Jesus, the Stone, will judge, or grind into powder, all who do not believe in Him. There are a few different interpretations of this verse, but no matter what, whoever does not believe in Jesus will not enter the kingdom and will be judged. Of that we can be sure!

Even though this parable is about the first century religious leaders rejecting the kingdom, there is still application for us today. We in the Church do not have an opportunity to accept or reject the kingdom as the first century Jews did. But we do have an opportunity to accept or reject Jesus as our Savior. Do not reject the Holy Spirit's conviction as the Jewish religious leaders rejected God's prophets and His Son. Believe that Jesus died for your sins and rose from the grave and He will give you eternal life.

Provoked thought

The kingdom of God will be taken from the first century Jews and given to a nation (the tribulation Jews) bearing the fruits of it. Those who rejected the chief cornerstone will be judged.

Chapter 28

The Parable of
the Wedding for a King's Son
Matthew 22:1-14

Audience
Chief priests, elders, Pharisees, anyone else in the temple (Matthew 21:23, 21:45-46).

Prompt
This parable immediately follows the parables of the two sons and the wicked vinedressers after the chief priests and elders of the people questioned Jesus' authority (Matthew 21:23).

Explanation
After telling the religious leaders the kingdom would be taken from them and given to the believing Jews of the tribulation (Matthew 21:43), Jesus tells this parable about who is invited to enter the kingdom and who will get in.

A king arranged a marriage for his son and sent out his servants to call those who were invited, but they would not come. He sent out more servants to tell those who were invited that everything for the wedding was ready. The invited made light of it and went their own ways. But some of the invitees seized the king's servants, treated them spitefully, and killed them. The king was furious when he heard about their treatment of his servants and sent out his armies to destroy them and burn their city.

He told his servants, "The wedding is ready, but those who were invited were not worthy. Therefore go into the highways, and as many as you find, invite to the wedding." The servants collected everyone they could, both bad and good, in the wedding hall. When the king came in, he noticed a guest without a wedding garment. The man did not know what to say when the king asked him how he came in without one. The king ordered the man to be bound hand and foot and cast into outer darkness.

While the provoked thought of this parable is about who will get into the kingdom, this parable also tells us how the kingdom will come. God repeatedly sent prophets to Israel to tell them how to enter the kingdom but they would not listen and "made light of it and went their ways" (Matthew 22:5). God eventually destroyed the first century Jews who rejected Jesus as well as Jerusalem, just like the invitees and their city are destroyed in the parable. One day the tribulation will begin and God will send 144,000 witnesses/servants to go into the whole world (the highways) and invite everyone to enter the kingdom by believing in Jesus (Revelation 7:4, Matthew 24:14). At the end of the tribulation, everyone will be gathered, both Jews and Gentiles, and their entrance into the kingdom will be based on their faith in Jesus (Matthew 25:31-46). Those without "wedding clothes" or faith will be cast into outer darkness and not enter the kingdom.

Jesus is making the point that Israel, during and before Jesus' first coming and preceding His second coming, are all called to enter the kingdom. They all were/will be given the opportunity to accept Him as King and Savior. Furthermore, before His second coming the whole world will be called. But few will accept the message. Few will be prepared with their "wedding clothes," or prepared by believing in Jesus. Few will be chosen by God to enter. What a humbling thought that something as wonderful as the kingdom will be rejected by so many. May we learn to be thankful for the salvation God has provided and be encouraged to tell others about the wedding feast to come so they will not miss it.

Provoked thought
Many are called, but few are chosen.

Chapter 29

The Parable of the Master Returning from a Wedding

Luke 12:35-38

Audience

Jesus is speaking to an innumerable multitude (Luke 12:1) but specifically the disciples (Luke 12:22).

Prompt

A man from the crowd tells Jesus to order his brother to divide the inheritance with him which prompts the parable of the rich fool. Jesus says in Luke 12:22, "Therefore I say to you, do not worry..." and then ends His discourse about not worrying by saying, "For where your treasure is, there your heart will be also" (Luke 12:34). This parable follows that conclusion.

Explanation

Jesus likens the crowd but specifically His disciples to be like men waiting for the return of their master from a wedding with their waist girded and their lamps burning. The master's servants are supposed to be watching, ready to open the door to his household immediately when he knocks, even if he comes during the night watches. The master will reward his watching servants by girding himself as a servant and serving them a meal.

Jesus is telling His disciples to watch and be ready for His coming. This parable is connected to the previous section in which Jesus tells His audience to not store up earthly treasure (parable of the rich fool) but seek the kingdom of God and not worry about earthly possessions (Luke 12:31). We are to be ready for the Son of Man because once He comes, there will not be time to build up our heavenly treasure. "Our soul is required of us" (Luke 12:20) because the Son of Man's coming is the time He will give rewards for our service. Our heavenly treasure will be weighed and there will be no more time to gather more.

This parable is told in the context of the Son of Man coming at the end of the tribulation as we will see more clearly in the parable of the wise and evil servants. When Jesus comes, He will reward those who survived the tribulation and they will enter the kingdom. This concept parallels how the Church should be ready for the rapture. Paul tells church age believers to watch and be sober in anticipation of Jesus coming for the Church (1 Thessalonians 5:6). For whatever generation experiences the rapture, they will be caught up and Jesus will give rewards for service (2 Corinthians 5:10).

In both cases, the coming of Jesus will happen at an unexpected time. For the tribulation, the Jews will not know the exact hour of His coming because it will be difficult to know when the seven year period began. It may also be hard to keep track of time given all the judgments that will take place. For the rapture, it is a signless event in which we can only guess when it will happen even though we will know the season.

Both the Jews and the Church have the same command: watch and be ready for we will be judged for our service. But before Jesus comes at each event, our waists should girded, meaning we are always working in service of Him. Our lamps should be burning, which means we should always be watching for His coming.

Provoked thought

Be ready, for the Son of Man is coming at an hour you do not expect.

Chapter 30

The Parable of
the Fig Tree

Matthew 24:32-33, Mark 13:28-29, Luke 21:29-31

Audience

The disciples, specifically Peter, James, John, and Andrew (Matthew 24:3, Mark 13:3).

Prompt

This is the first parable in the Olivet discourse which is prompted by the disciples asking "When will these things be? And what will be the sign of your coming, and of the end of the age?" (Matthew 24:3). These questions are all asking the same thing: what signs will precede Jesus' second coming?

Explanation

When the branches of the fig tree, or any tree, become tender, start budding, and put forth leaves, it means it is springtime, which also means summer is near.

In the Olivet Discourse, Jesus is talking about the generation that will go through the tribulation. This parable applies to them even though it is the disciples that are the audience. Jesus is relating the nearness of His coming and the events of the tribulation to the budding of the fig tree. If springtime, made apparent by the budding of the tree, is here, then you know summertime is close. Likewise, if the events of the tribulation are happening, you know Jesus' coming is close.

While it is not part of the provoked thought, Jesus gives the assurance that this generation, the one *about* whom He is speaking not the one *to* whom He is speaking, will not pass away till all these things take place (Matthew 24:34). This means the tribulation will not span multiple generations and at least some of that generation will survive the tribulation.

This parable does not apply directly to the Church, but as with many parables the principle can be applied to our age. The rapture is a signless event and does not need to be preceded by anything. So when we see things that are preparing the world for the events of the tribulation, such as the world being brought closer to a one world government or a one world economy, the rapture must be drawing near. On the other hand, the preparation for the tribulation could last a very long time. Jesus will come when He is ready and we must wait patiently. Even though world events make it seem as if the rapture is very near, it may not be. Until then, we have a job to do for God before we are called home.

Provoked thought
When you see all the events of the tribulation, know that Christ's second coming is near – at the doors!

Chapter 31

The Parable of the Master Going Away

Mark 13:34

Audience

The disciples, specifically Peter, James, John, and Andrew (Matthew 24:3, Mark 13:3).

Prompt

This parable is told in the Olivet Discourse after Jesus explains that no one knows the time Jesus is returning.

Explanation

A man went to a far away country, giving authority to his servants and to each his work. He commanded the doorkeeper to watch for his return.

This parable is likened to how the tribulation generation is supposed to watch and pray because they do not know when Christ will return. A servant would not want to be caught sleeping on the job when his master returns. Likewise, the tribulation generation should be working, watching, and praying because the exact time of day when Jesus returns is unknown. When Jesus does return, He will return suddenly and there will not be time to accomplish any more work.

Even though this parable is for the generation in the tribulation, we in the Church should be working, watching, and praying because we don't know when Jesus will return for us (the rapture). We should always watch for His return as the tribulation generation watches for His second coming.

Provoked thought
Take heed, watch and pray; for you do not know when the time of Jesus' return is.

Chapter 32

The Parable of
the Master and the Thief

Matthew 24:43, Luke 12:39

Audience

In Luke, Jesus is speaking to an innumerable multitude (Luke 12:1) but specifically the disciples (Luke 12:22).

In Matthew, the disciples, specifically Peter, James, John, and Andrew (Matthew 24:3, Mark 13:3).

Prompt

In Luke, this parable immediately follows the parable of the master returning from a wedding. In fact, it would be easy to see these parables as part of the same story if it were not for Matthew's account that only tells the parable of the master and the thief.

In Matthew, this parable is told in the Olivet Discourse during the section in which Jesus is explaining that no one knows the day and hour when He is coming back (Matthew 24:36).

Explanation

In this parable, Jesus explains that if a master of a house knows when a thief is coming, he would watch his estate and not allow it to be broken into.

Jesus is using this parable as another way of telling the disciples to be ready. The details of the parable do not have a direct correlation to the disciples, Jesus, Satan, or anything similiar. The story is simply using the example of a thief coming to a house and his ability to break in is determined by whether the master is watching or not.

No one wants to be robbed, so proper defenses should be put in place to deter thieves. If the master of the house is always expecting an attack, the thief cannot break in unexpectedly. Thieves do not notify their victims when they are going to attack, so a master must always be ready to deter or stop the attack.

In Matthew's telling of this parable, Jesus is clearly speaking about the generation of Jews in the tribulation, telling them to be ready for the Son of Man coming back to start His kingdom. Both Matthew and Luke's telling are exactly the same, and end with the same phrase "Therefore you also be ready, for the Son of Man is coming at an hour you do not expect." We know both tellings must be talking about Jesus coming back at the end of the tribulation.

From our perspective, it is a bit odd for Jesus to say in Matthew 24:36, "But of that day and hour no one knows, not even the angels of heaven, but My Father only" because there are so many signs during the tribulation that precede Jesus' arrival. But deception will be so great that many will not recognize the signs. That is why Jesus starts the Olivet Discourse by saying, "Take heed that no one deceives you" (Matthew 24:4). Furthermore, the conditions of the tribulation will be very extreme and the passage of time may be very difficult to keep track of. Jesus says to watch the signs, not the calendar.

For instance, the signing of the peace treaty between the Antichrist and Israel probably will happen before its announcement to the world, so it will be difficult to know exactly when the seventieth week of Daniel begins (Daniel 9:27). The changes in the sun, moon, stars, and sky in seal judgment six could make the passing of day to night difficult to interpret and we don't know how long this will last (Revelation 6:12-14). When a third of the sun, moon, and stars are darkened, this adds to the difficulty of knowing when days are passing and again we don't know how long this will last (Revelation 8:12). Bowl number five causes darkness right after the sun scorches men in bowl four (Revelation 16:8, 10). How many days will be darkened we don't know.

Because of these and many other judgments, people might not go outside much (if they are allowed outside by the Antichrist's government) and might instead stay in places with no windows. The conditions of the tribulation will be so extreme that we can imagine how finding food and water is more important than counting down the days before Jesus arrives. Furthermore, will Jesus come back seven years from the peace treaty according to the Jewish calendar, which has 360 days, or according to the Gregorian calendar which most of the world uses now? I would think it would be according to the Jewish calendar, which would make it even harder to know the exact date of His return using the Gregorian calendar. The signs of the tribulation, not the calendar, show how close it is to His return.

This parable is about being ready for Jesus' second coming, and as explained in the parable of the master returning from a wedding, the Church is given parallel commands to watch and be ready for His coming at the rapture (I Thessalonians 5:6). We are to be ready just like the tribulation Jews even though we are waiting for a different event. Jesus is not going to notify anyone when He is coming back for either event, so we must also always be ready as a master is always watching for a thief.

Provoked thought

Be ready, for the Son of Man is coming at an hour you do not expect.

Chapter 33

The Parable of
the Wise and Evil Servants

Matthew 24:45-51, Luke 12:42-48

Audience

In Luke, Jesus is speaking to an innumerable multitude (Luke 12:1) but specifically the disciples (Luke 12:22).

In Matthew, the disciples, specifically Peter, James, John, and Andrew (Matthew 24:3, Mark 13:3).

Prompt

In Luke, Peter asks Jesus whether He is speaking the parables of the master returning from a wedding and the master and the thief to only the disciples or to the multitude (Luke 12:41).

In Matthew, this parable is told after the parable of the master and the thief in the Olivet Discourse during the section in which Jesus is explaining that no one knows the day and hour when He is coming back (Matthew 24:36).

Because of the difference in prompts, I believe Jesus told this parable at least twice (He could have told it other times that weren't recorded by the Gospel authors). One evidence of this is the change of verb tense between Matthew 24:45 and Luke 12:42. In Luke, the master "will make" the servant ruler of the household, but in Matthew the master already "made" him ruler.

In the Luke telling, the tribulation has not happened yet according to the context in which Jesus is speaking. However, when the parable is told during the Olivet Discourse, the tribulation has already happened and Jesus is giving parables explaining how people will act throughout the tribulation. While this example might be stretching the text too far, I believe it is still apparent that Luke and Matthew recorded different tellings of this parable.

Explanation

After using the parable of the master and thief to tell His disciples to be ready, Jesus tells a parable that asks what kind of person a disciple will be: faithful and wise or evil? A faithful and wise servant will be made ruler over the master's house, goods, and all he has. That kind of servant will give food to his fellow servants. That servant will be blessed if he is doing these things when the master arrives.

However, if that servant is evil, realizing his master is delayed in his coming, he will not be watching for his master. He will beat his fellow servants and live a drunken lifestyle. Because that kind of servant is not watching even though he knew he was supposed to be, the master will come on a day he is not expecting and will judge him harshly as a hypocrite. That servant will weep and gnash his teeth from this judgment.

Jesus is giving the picture of two kinds of people in this parable, one that will enter the kingdom and one that will not. One person is watching for Jesus' return and is working as he should by serving his fellow servants. Both the faithful and evil servants have fellow servants. I believe the servants are the Jewish people, which fits the context of the Olivet Discourse. Since this parable is told about people during the tribulation, we know one example of the kind of person waiting for Jesus' return are the 144,000 witnesses.

While faith isn't explicitly mentioned in this parable, we know entrance into the kingdom is conditioned on faith and not works (Matthew 8:10-13). We can then infer from this parable and the other parables in the Olivet Discourse that believers/ servants will care for each other during the tribulation and this work will be rewarded. It seems the circumstances of the tribulation will force this behavior to happen when someone believes.

In the sheep and the goats judgment in Matthew 25:31-46, Jesus does not point out the faith of the sheep but rather their works. However, if only their works mattered as far as how to get into the kingdom that would contradict every passage in the Bible that conditions entrance into the kingdom/heaven on faith alone in Christ alone (John 5:24, 6:40). I believe the idea being alluded to is that during the tribulation, placing your faith in Christ will manifest itself in works because of the circumstances of the tribulation. God does not force works nor are the automatic but having faith will in some way show in a work, such as taking care of one of the 144,000 Jewish witnesses. This person will be blessed when Jesus comes in at least one way by entering the kingdom after surviving the tribulation.

On the other hand, the evil servant, an unbeliever, will not be watching for Jesus' return but will instead beat his fellow servants or other Jews. What the evil and wicked servant is doing may be one cause of the vast amount of martyrdom in the tribulation (Revelation 6:9-11). He will also eat, drink, get drunk, and most likely have a generally careless lifestyle. This servant knew he was supposed to be watching for Jesus' return but did not prepare for His arrival.

But one day Jesus will come back. The mention of "weeping and gnashing of teeth" means this unaware servant will not enter the kingdom, receiving his portion with the hypocrites.

When Jesus says he will be "cut in two" and "beaten with many stripes," I believe this is a picture of the torment that will be experienced by those outside the kingdom.

In Luke's telling, Jesus' adds another type of evil servant who was unaware that his master was coming back. This person, who doesn't know to be watching for Jesus' return, will not have as severe a punishment as the person who did know. This indicates the punishment for unbelievers will be fair according to their knowledge and actions.

Jesus concludes the telling in Luke with the principle that more responsibility is upon those to whom more has been given. This is a general principle that is easily applied, but we can also break this principle down for both the believer and unbeliever and their relationship to God. To believers of whom God has given more knowledge, talents and abilities, God will require more from them. They have both more to gain and more to lose when they are judged (see the parable of the minas). Conversely, unbelievers will be judged based on what God gave them in terms of their chances to believe and their actions (Luke 12:46-47, Revelation 20:12).

Jesus also says "to whom much has been committed, of him they will ask the more" (Luke 12:48). This is also an easily applied principle, and we will break it down for believers but not unbelievers for God will not commit anything to them. For believers, God will commit things, people, ministries, etc. But as He commits things to us, He will continually ask for more service. Even though the burden can be greater with more service, we should be grateful that God wants to continually use us for His glory. At the end of our life we should be able to say "I have fought the good fight, I have finished the race, I have kept the faith" (2 Timothy 4:7).

Reader, are you going to be a faithful and wise servant or an evil servant?

Provoked thought

Matthew: A faithful and wise person will be watching and working while Jesus is delaying His coming but and evil person will not be watching and behaving badly. Both will be judged accordingly.

Luke: Everyone to whom much is given, from him much will be required; and to whom much has been committed, of him they will ask the more.

Chapter 34

The Parable of the Ten Virgins

Matthew 25:1-13

Audience
The disciples, specifically Peter, James, John, and Andrew (Matthew 24:3, Mark 13:3).

Prompt
This parable follows the parable of the wise and evil servants in the Olivet discourse which is prompted by the disciples asking "When will these things be? And what will be the sign of your coming, and of the end of the age?" (Matthew 24:3). These questions are all asking the same thing: what signs will precede Jesus' second coming?

Explanation
Ten virgins, five wise and five foolish, took their lamps and went out to meet the bridegroom. But the bridegroom was delayed and the virgins slept. At midnight a cry was heard: "Behold, the bridegroom is coming; go out to meet him!" The virgins lit their lamps. The wise virgins, who were prepared and brought plenty of oil, had no trouble lighting their lamps. The foolish virgins did not have enough oil and their lamps were going out. They asked the wise virgins to share some of their oil, but there was not enough to split between everyone. The foolish virgins left to

buy more oil. While they were buying, the bridegroom came and the wise virgins went in with him to the wedding, and the door was shut. When the foolish virgins returned they called for the bridegroom to open the door. But he responded saying, "Assuredly, I say to you, I do not know you."

This parable is about being prepared for Jesus' return at the end of the tribulation. Jesus says to watch and be ready like the wise virgins. In order to "be ready," the tribulation generation must believe in Jesus as their Savior like the wise virgins had to have their lamps burning.

There will be those during the tribulation who know Jesus will return but do not place their faith in Him. The foolish virgins went out to meet the bridegroom but were not prepared to enter the wedding because they did not take enough oil with them. It was too late for them to get more oil when the cry was heard. Some people in the tribulation will put off believing in Jesus even though they know He is coming. Whatever alerts them that His arrival is here, like the cry in the parable, it will be too late to believe.

This parable directly applies to the tribulation generation, not the Church. However, there is a parallel to our age. The rapture is a signless event, meaning it does not have any signs preceding it. We don't know when it will happen and it could even happen today! We should not wait to believe in Jesus because the tribulation will be a horrible time to be on earth. We should believe in Him now so that we are rescued from that time (among many other reasons!). The rapture is called the "blessed hope" (Titus 2:13) and what a blessing it will be to be spared from the worst time in earth's history!

Provoked thought

Watch, for you know neither the day nor the hour in which the Son of Man is coming.

Chapter 35

The Parable of the Talents

Matthew 25:14-30

Audience

The disciples, specifically Peter, James, John, and Andrew (Matthew 24:3, Mark 13:3).

Prompt

This parable follows the parable of the ten virgins in the Olivet discourse which is prompted by the disciples asking "When will these things be? And what will be the sign of your coming, and of the end of the age?" (Matthew 24:3). These questions are all asking the same thing: what signs will precede Jesus' second coming?

Explanation

The parable of the talents is about what people should do with the abilities God gave them, namely their ability to believe in Jesus Christ.

Before a man left to a far away country, he called his own servants and delivered his goods to them. He gave one five talents, one two, and one one. He gave them differing amounts according to their ability. Then he left.

The man returned after a long time and settled accounts with his servants. The servant with five talents gained five more, and entered into the joy of his lord. The servant with two talents gained two more and also entered into the joy of his lord. The servant with one talent was afraid of the man and hid his talent in the ground. The master told the wicked and lazy servant that he should have deposited the money in the bank so he would have received back his own with interest. The talent was taken from him and he was cast into outer darkness where there will be weeping and gnashing of teeth.

Just like the parable of the minas, this parable parallels Jesus' going into heaven and returning. However, there are many differences between the parables even though they sound similiar.

In this parable, each servant is given a different amount of talents. In the parable of the minas each servant is given the same amount: one mina. The wicked servant is cast into outer darkness in the talents while only the mina is taken from him in the minas parable. Therefore, the servants in this parable must not all be believers. The talents have an impact on earned rewards but also entrance into heaven. There is also no mention of the citizens that are slain in this parable.

I believe the talents are the abilities God gives us, the ability of faith and any other abilities.

The first "talent" that God gives everyone is the ability to believe (some people do not have the mental capacity to believe because of some disorder or deformation. It is beyond the scope of this book to talk about these cases, but I believe God's grace covers them and they are in heaven. For God would not punish a person by sending them to hell without giving them the ability to believe.). The reason the servant with one talent was not admitted into the joy of his lord is because he did not use his God-given ability to believe in Jesus Christ. His talent is given to the servant who had ten talents. In this way, the unused ability abundantly benefits the person who already has rewards. The parable does not give us the details of how this redistribution works, but we know that from him who does not have, even what he has will be taken away.

For the good and faithful servants, they used their "talents" to gain more. They first used their ability to believe and they were given eternal life. Then they performed good works by faith that earned rewards. Apparently the things we are faithful over on earth are few compared to the things we will be given authority over in eternity. Even though God gave each servant differing amounts of abilities, each servant used the talents to produce the potential of what was possible to earn. Likewise, when we use our full potential God gave us, we will have done what was our duty to do (Luke 17:10). We will not have a prideful attitude about our accomplishments, but praise God because we know He is the one who enabled us to earn the rewards.

We have no way of knowing how many "talents" God has given us. All we can do is be faithful with what He has given and follow His leading wherever He may go.

Provoked thought
To everyone who has, more will be given, and he will have abundance; but from him who does not have, even what he has will be taken away.

Chapter 36

The Parable of
the Minas

Luke 19:11-27

Audience

Luke does not define the audience clearly. The parable takes place after Zacchaeus was converted (Luke 19:1-10). Most likely at least the disciples were present.

Prompt

Jesus spoke this parable because He was near Jerusalem and the people with Him thought the kingdom of God would appear immediately (Luke 19:11).

Explanation

The parable of the minas is about what believers should be doing with their lives while they are waiting for Jesus to return at His second coming. With His coming the kingdom will begin.

Before a nobleman left for a far country to receive a kingdom, he called ten of his servants and delivered to them ten minas. He said to them, "Do business till I come." But the citizens of the nobleman hated him and did not want him to reign over them. When he returned after receiving the kingdom, he called his ten servants to whom he had given minas to testify how much every man had gained by trading.

The first man earned ten minas. The second earned five minas. Both were given authority over cities, ten and five respectively, because of faithful and good service. But another servant came and confessed that he hid the mina because of fear of the nobleman. The nobleman judged him by his own words, that he was a wicked servant, not even putting the mina in the bank to collect interest. The mina was taken from the wicked servant and given to the servant who earned ten. Then the nobleman ordered the citizens who did not want him as king to be brought before him and slain.

Before discussing what the mina is, we can define other parts of the parable. Even though it is not the provoked thought of the parable, Jesus is using this parable to tell His audience the kingdom will not begin when He reaches Jerusalem. Israel will reject Him, just like the citizens rejected the nobleman. Jesus will leave for heaven and receive a kingdom like the nobleman leaves to a far away country and receives a kingdom. When Jesus returns He will judge and slay those who hated and did not believe in Him just like the nobleman. But while Jesus is gone, His servants have a job to do like the nobleman's servants were supposed to do business.

In this parable, each servant is given the same amount, one mina. This is different from the parable of the talents in which each servant is given differing amounts. Also, the wicked servant is not cast into outer darkness as he is in the parable of the talents, but only the mina is taken from him. Therefore, the servants in this parable are all believers and are earning rewards with their minas. In the parable of the talents how the servants use their talent not only determines rewards, but also entrance into heaven.

I believe the best way to understand the mina is the one life God gives each of us.

We should be "doing business" with our lives until Jesus returns. With our "mina," we all have the potential to earn rewards during our life. Each servant calls the mina they received "your mina" meaning the nobleman's. Likewise, we should recognize the life we have been given is from God. With it, the more we invest in heavenly things the more authority we will be given in heaven. Any servant that invests his "mina" will be a good and faithful servant.

On the other hand, there will be believers who do not produce a profit with their life. In the parable, the wicked servant feared the nobleman because he was a harsh man, collecting what he did not deposit and reaping what he did not sow. The nobleman does not deny this about himself. Instead, he says the servant should have put the mina in the bank to collect interest. If believers fear God as the servant did, they can still give their resources or money to another believer who will do something productive with it. At least then there will be "interest," or a profit for God from the believer rather than the believer producing nothing with his life.

The wicked servant's mina is given to the servant who earned ten minas. What the wicked servant could have earned but didn't is given to another. The principle we learn is there will be people in heaven who earn no rewards and what they could have earned will be given to others who already have rewards. They will still enter heaven because the wicked servant is not said to be cast into outer darkness. He does not have any additional rewards but even what he has will be taken from him.

The other servants in the parable seem to think this is unfair but from God's perspective it is fair. The Bible says many times God will render to every one according to his work (Psalm 62:12, Proverbs 24:12, Revelation 22:12). God will not reward anyone if they do not deserve it. Therefore it makes sense that even what they could have earned will be taken away and given to another. Reader, do not be like the wicked servant; use your "mina" wisely.

Provoked thought

Everyone who has will be given; and from him who does not have, even what he has will be taken away from him.

Section 3

General Parables

Chapter 37

The Parable of
the Blind Leading the Blind

Luke 6:39

Audience
Multitudes and disciples (Luke 6:19-20).

Prompt
This parable is in the "judge not" portion of Luke's account of the Sermon on the Mount. Jesus is teaching the multitudes many things about righteousness.

Explanation
Jesus asks if the blind can lead the blind. The assumed answer is no, because neither can see where they are going. Next, Jesus asks if the blind were to lead the blind, won't they both fall into a ditch? The assumed answer to this question is yes for the same reason: they cannot see where they are going.

Jesus follows this short parable by saying, "A disciple is not above his teacher, but everyone who is perfectly trained will be like his teacher" (Luke 6:40). Then He explains how it is hypocritical to talk about a speck in a brother's eye while we have a plank in our own. This all relates to Jesus saying, "Judge not, and you shall not be judged" (Luke 6:37).

A blind man cannot see; therefore he cannot lead others along a path. In the same way, a man with a plank cannot see clearly to see a speck in someone else's eye. If a man with a plank was to point out a speck in his brothers' eye, both would "fall into a ditch." The brother could call the man a hypocrite because he sees the plank in his eye, yet he has a speck in his own, and is also being a hypocrite for pointing out the man's plank! Both are judging each other in an improper way and "falling into a ditch." Falling into a ditch is a bad situation but it can be corrected; one way or another you can climb out. However, every person that falls in would rather not have in the first place.

Jesus gives the answer of how to not be blind and "remove the plank from your own eye." When we are a disciple of a Teacher (assumed to be Jesus), we should not try to be above Him, but be trained by Him. When we are perfectly trained or thoroughly complete, we will be like our Teacher. The disciple of this Teacher will know how to identify his "blindness" or "planks," and correct his vision before correcting the "specks" in his brother's eye. In this way, he will not be blind and avoid leading anyone, whether they are blind or not, into a ditch.

Notice that Jesus assumes we will have things that obscure our vision. Notice also that Jesus does not say we should never correct a brother, but we should be able to "see clearly" before we do (Luke 6:42). Jesus is not saying never judge, but only judge after being perfectly trained to see clearly. And by what measure should we judge? The same measure of judgment that we learned from the Teacher (Luke 6:38, 40). Therefore, if we use judgments that are outside God's Word, we are not judging correctly and have not removed our plank.

Provoked thought
A man who cannot see clearly cannot correctly lead others and will lead himself and them into a bad situation.

Chapter 38

The Parable of
Pearls before Swine

Matthew 7:6

Audience
Multitudes and disciples (Matthew 5:1).

Prompt
This parable is in the "judge not" portion of Matthew's account of the Sermon on the Mount. Jesus is teaching the multitudes many things about righteousness.

Explanation
This parable is told after the parable of the blind leading the blind and Jesus calling those who judge with a plank in their eye hypocrites. Jesus says, "Do not give what is holy to the dogs, not cast your pearls before swine" (Matthew 7:6). This is Hebrew parallelism, in which both examples mean the same thing. Jesus says the swine will trample your pearls "under their feet, and turn and tear you in pieces."

Jesus is giving another picture that parallels the blind falling into a ditch. The basic idea of this parable is not giving something valuable to something detestable. Swine were unclean animals to the Jews. They would have recoiled at the thought of throwing something as valuable as pearls into a swine pen. But this is exactly what happens when we judge a brother with a speck while we have a plank.

When you judge outside of God's judgment, you are judging the law and boasting a higher position than God (James 4:11-12). We have created a law unto ourselves which has no standard except the measure we use. When we hypocritically judge, we are throwing our "pearls," our character or who we are, before "swine." A fellow brother, noticing the plank in our eye, can "trample under his feet" this judgment by pointing our the plank. He now can "turn and tear us in pieces," ruining our character, judgment, position, or whatever quality about us he wants. This trampling and tearing to pieces is parallel to the blind falling in a ditch.

We pointed out in the previous parable that one way or another a ditch can be climbed out of. Wounds from a "swine attack" can be healed unless the wounds are fatal. Using these two parables, Jesus gives us a vivid picture of what happens when we judge hypocritically. The relationship between us and a brother could be healed, but we could also lose that brother permanently. It is far better to make sure we are a perfectly trained disciple, not a blind man casting pearls before swine.

Provoked thought
When you judge hypocritically, you are casting your character before men who can ruin you.

Chapter 39

The Parable of
the Good Tree, Good Fruit

Matthew 7:16-18 & 12:33, Luke 6:43-45

Audience

Multitudes (Matthew 12:23, Luke 6:17).

Prompt

Jesus tells this parable in Matthew's account of the Sermon on the Mount after a warning to beware of false prophets. In Matthew 12, Pharisees attributed Jesus' ability to cast out demons to Beelzebub. This parable follows Jesus talking about the blasphemy against the Holy Spirit.

In Luke, this parable occurs during Luke's account of the Sermon on the Mount after the parable of the blind leading the blind.

Explanation

You know whether a tree is good or bad by whether the fruit is good or bad. A good tree does not bear bad fruit, nor does a bad tree bear good fruit. A good tree has good fruit and bad tree has bad fruit. Men do not gather figs from thorns, nor do they gather grapes from a bramble bush. Bad trees are cut down and thrown into the fire.

In each Gospel, this parable has the same meaning, but in

Matthew's Gospel it is directed at the Pharisees. In Luke's Gospel, Jesus explains it in a more general sense.

A good tree will produce good fruit because the tree itself is good. Likewise, a man who is inwardly good will bring forth good. What is the good? Words (Matthew 12:34). A man who has a good heart will speak good words. A bad tree will produce bad fruit because the tree itself is bad. A man who has a bad heart will speak bad words. Whatever you treasure in your heart, good or bad, will be how you talk.

The Pharisees were "bad trees" because they spoke bad things. In fact, this "brood of vipers" were not capable of speaking good things because they were so evil. They spoke out of the abundance of their heart. Jesus continues to explain that we will be judged for our words (Matthew 12:36). Words are very powerful; we can bless and curse out of the same mouth (James 3:9). We should be very careful how we talk because our speech reveals our heart (Matthew 12:34).

Words are so revealing that we can know who people are by them. In Matthew's account of the Sermon on the Mount, this parable is a picture of how to know "wolves in sheep's clothing." Outwardly, men may appear to be sheep, meaning that they will look like sheep and do good things. But inwardly, they are wolves or bad trees. How do you know the difference? By their fruit. What is fruit? Words.

The most common interpretation of this parable in the Sermon on the Mount is that Christians are supposed to be "fruit inspectors," inspecting other's works to determine whether they are saved or not. This parable actually teaches the opposite. Those that are wolves will look like those that are sheep which means unsaved people will look like saved people. They will look and act the same. We can only tell the difference between a wolf in sheep's clothing and a real sheep by what they say, not by how they look or act.

Directly following this parable in Matthew 7:21, Jesus says, "Not everyone who says to me, 'Lord, Lord,' shall enter the kingdom of heaven." Who are the ones that don't enter? The wolves in sheep's clothing. Who does enter? "He who does the will of My father in heaven." What is this "will of the Father" that would make someone a sheep or a good tree? We find it in John 6:40:

> And this is the will of Him who sent Me, that everyone who sees the Son and believes in Him may have everlasting life; and I will raise him up at the last day.
> *John 6:40*

Faith in Jesus Christ is what allows a person to enter the kingdom of heaven. The ones who don't have faith will not enter.

The wolves in sheep's clothing, who do not have faith, will appeal to Jesus on judgment day to look at the many wonders they did in His name (Matthew 7:22). They are telling the truth because they looked like and did the same thing as sheep. But, because they don't have faith, Jesus will declare to them, "I never knew you; depart from me, you who practice lawlessness!" (Matthew 7:23). How did they practice lawlessness when they looked and acted like sheep? By their words and actions without faith (Hebrews 11:6)! Their words revealed they were a bad tree. Bad trees, people without faith, are sent to hell like a bad tree is cut down and thrown into the fire.

We can see that inspecting someone's works to determine whether they are saved is not what we should be doing. We should be inspecting their words to determine whether what they say is good or bad.

Knowing a person's heart by their words informs our response to them. If the words they speak indicate they aren't saved, we should find ways to share the Gospel with them. If we can tell by their words they are a believer, we should treat them as a brother or sister in Christ! If their words indicate they are saved but they are not acting in a way that is pleasing to God, we should encourage, correct, comfort, or whatever is proper as one believer should do for another believer. If their words don't reveal whether they are saved or not, we can never go wrong sharing the Gospel!

Just as we pay attention to someone else's words, we should pay attention to our words for we will be judged by them; not for salvation but for rewards (Matthew 12:36-37). We can sometimes trick ourselves by concealing our true motives and justifying ourselves, but our words reveal our heart. If our first response to something is bad, but we stop ourselves from saying it, our heart has just been revealed. "So speak and so do as those who will be judged by the law of liberty" (James 2:12).

Provoked thought
By their fruits you will know people's hearts, for out of the abundance of the heart the mouth speaks.

Chapter 40

The Parable of the Wise and Foolish Men

Matthew 7:24-27, Luke 6:47-49

Audience

Multitudes (Matthew 5:1, Luke 6:19).

Prompt

This parable follows the parable of the good tree, good fruit in the Sermon on the Mount.

Explanation

Whoever hears the sayings of Jesus and does them is like a wise man who built his house on the rock. When the rain, wind, and floods came and beat vehemently against the house, they could not shake it. The house did not fall for it was founded on the rock. But whoever hears the sayings of Jesus and do not do them is like a foolish man who built his house on the sand or earth without a foundation. When the rain, wind, and flood came, they beat vehemently against it, and the house fell immediately with a great fall.

In Luke's Gospel, this parable is preceded by Jesus asking the multitude, "Why do you call me 'Lord, Lord,' and not do the things which I say?" (Luke 6:46). In Matthew's Gospel He begins the parable with the word "therefore." Jesus is referencing the teaching He just gave that not everyone who says "Lord, Lord" will enter the kingdom of heaven (Matthew 7:21). But by using the word "therefore" and referencing His sayings, He is also summarizing His entire discourse and the two kinds of people that were listening.

If someone hears Jesus's teachings and does them, which starts with believing in Him for salvation (John 6:40), they are like a wise man who builds his house on a rock. The rock provides a solid foundation for his house that weather will not easily destroy. When storms do come, the foundation of the house protects the walls and roof from moving.

The foundation is what provides the house stability, not the walls and roof. Jesus' sayings are stable and doing them provides a person stability when troubles come. Notice that a person who does Jesus' sayings does not necessarily avoid trouble. But when trouble comes, Jesus' sayings are what protects a person's "house" or life from falling.

However, if a person hears Jesus' sayings and does not do them, which means they haven't believed in Him as Savior or followed Him as a disciple, they are like a foolish man who builds his house on the sand or earth. Neither of these, especially sand, provide any stability on which the house will rest. The foundation of the house is very unstable. When storms come, rain and floods will move earth and sand especially if there is a strong wind. When the foundation moves, the house will go with it. The fall will be great because there won't be a house to live in anymore but only a pile of materials on the ground.

Building a foundation on anything but Jesus' sayings will cause destruction when tribulations arise because there is nothing to keep a person stable. Their "house" or life will have to be rebuilt continually. They may try change after change to their life that will create stability, but without believing and doing Jesus' sayings they will never have a solid foundation.

This goes a bit beyond the parable, but you cannot do Jesus' sayings without hearing them. How do you hear them? The Bible is the only source. If you are not reading the Bible or hearing someone teach it correctly, then you do not know what Jesus' sayings are. Without knowing them, you can't "build your house" or live your life with a solid foundation. Reader, please make Scripture a part of your life so that you will have stability when troubles come.

Provoked thought
Hearing and doing Jesus' sayings provides a stable foundation in times of trouble. Hearing and not doing Jesus' sayings provides no foundation at all.

Chapter 41

The Parable of the Children in the Marketplace

Matthew 11:16-17, Luke 7:31-32

Audience

All the people (Luke 7:29) or multitudes (Matthew 11:7).

Prompt

John the Baptist sent some of his disciples to ask whether Jesus was the coming One (Matthew 11:2-3, Luke 7:18-20). Jesus praised John's ministry (Matthew 11:7-15, Luke 7:24-28) and the people justified God. But the Pharisees and lawyers rejected the will of God because they were not baptized (Luke 7:28-29).

Explanation

The Jews in the first century are like children sitting in the marketplaces calling to one other. They are saying, "We played the flute for you and you did not dance, we mourned to you and you did not lament and weep."

Jesus is telling this parable to compare how the Pharisees and lawyers treated John and Himself even though their behavior was different. In the parable, the companions of the children do not dance, mourn, or weep when the other children played the flute and mourned. The companions did what they wanted to do and responded the same to both things even though the actions of the children should have elicited different responses.

Likewise, the Pharisees and lawyers responded to John and Jesus the same even though they acted different. John was abstinent from basically all norms of society. Jesus indulged in society by eating and drinking. He also was around everyone from tax collectors and sinners to the religious leaders. John preached a baptism in preparation of the Messiah, and Jesus preached accepting Him as the Messiah. The Pharisees and Lawyers did not respond to either one just like the companions of the children in the marketplace. They rejected both messages and the messengers.

Jesus ends the explanation of the parable by saying "Wisdom is justified by (all) her children" (Matthew 11:19, Luke 7:35). Those who are wise will justify wisdom by being wise. Wisdom is validated in the end by those who do the right thing. Both Jesus and John were correct in their message that Jesus is the Messiah and long awaited King. Even if it doesn't seem correct now, those who were wise and believed their message acted correctly and one day there will be proof this was the wise thing to do.

The Pharisees and lawyers believed what they wanted and were not swayed by John or Jesus' message no matter what signs they were given. They were not wise and found reasons to validate what they already thought instead of humbling themselves to change their mind. They believed what they wanted to believe not matter who "played the flute" or "mourned." If someone does not want to believe something, they will find a reason to keep from believing it no matter what is happening around them.

Provoked thought

The wise will prove what is correct by being wise. Wisdom is justified by all her children.

Chapter 42

The Parable of the Rich Fool

Luke 12:16-21

Audience
Innumerable multitude (Luke 12:1).

Prompt
A man from the crowd tells Jesus to order his brother to divide the inheritance with him (Luke 12:13).

Explanation
In this parable, Jesus tells the story of a rich man who had a very abundant yield from his fields. The man thought about what he should do with the crops since he did not have enough storage. He decided to tear down his barns and build bigger barns in which to store his crops so that he would not have to work any longer. "But God said to him, 'Fool! This night your soul will be required of you; then whose will those things be which you have provided?'"

This parable is preceded by Jesus telling the crowd, "Take heed and beware of covetousness, for one's life does not consist in the abundance of the things he possesses" (Luke 12:15). This parable is a way to illustrate that point and address the man who demanded his brother divide the inheritance.

The man who wanted part of the inheritance was coveting or being greedy for earthly wealth. In the parable, the rich man presumably had more wealth than the man in the crowd and had gained so much that he thought he no longer needed to work. However, the man would die the night he decided this, which is what is meant by "your soul will be required of you" (Luke 12:20). Who would own his possessions after his death? Certainly not the rich man. We know from Ecclesiastes 2:18-19 that it is vanity that we must leave all we have worked for to men who will come after us. And we don't know whether they will take care of our possessions or ruin them!

Jesus makes the same point as Solomon by saying, "So is he who lays up treasure for himself, and is not rich toward God" (Luke 12:21). Since we all die and our possessions do not come with us into eternity, what is the value of our earthly treasure? Nothing. It is vanity.

Both the rich fool and Solomon in Ecclesiastes said we should eat, drink, and be merry. But the fool said to "take [his] ease," which means to not work (Luke 12:19). Even though your earthly possessions are worthless compared to heavenly possessions, Solomon never says to stop working. God gave us work to exercise, occupy, and test us (Ecclesiastes 1:13, 2:10, 2:18). But we are to "enjoy the good of all our labor" because "it is a gift of God" (Ecclesiastes 2:13). Paul wrote in Colossians 3:17, "whatever you do in word or deed, do all in the name of the Lord Jesus, giving thanks to God the Father through Him."

Therefore do not be greedy for earthly possessions, but "lay up for yourselves treasures in heaven" (Matthew 6:20). How do we store up treasures in heaven? Walk by faith and in the works that God prepared for us (2 Corinthians 5:7, Ephesians 2:10).

Provoked thought

Take heed and beware of covetousness, for one's life does not consist in the abundance of the things he possesses.

Chapter 43

The Parable of
the Wedding Invitees
Luke 14:7-11

Audience
Invitees at the house of one of the rulers of the Pharisees (Luke 14:1).

Prompt
Jesus healed a man who had dropsy after asking the dinner invitees if it was lawful to heal on the Sabbath (Luke 14:2-6). He then spoke this parable when He noted how the invitees chose the best places to sit (Luke 14:7).

Explanation
In Jewish culture, seats at the table were ranked to show honor or how distinguished a guest was. The "best places" were in relation to the master of the feast, and it was clear which places were the most honorable. Jesus doesn't say where He was sitting in terms of His place, but my guess is that it was not the most honorable one.

In the parable, Jesus says to not take the best place, lest there is one more honorable invited. If the more honorable person arrives while there is someone in his seat, that person will be shamed by the host to give up that seat and move to the lowest place. Jesus says to take the lowest place so that the host will move you up to a better place and this will produce glory in the presence of those at the feast.

Unlike many of the parables, this parable is direct instruction to the hearers and has a simple point about pride and humbleness. The guests of the Pharisees all chose the best places as they arrived at the dinner just as they would have chosen the best places at a wedding in which they were invited. We don't know each person's exact motive for taking the best place, whether it was to show off to other guests, an inward attitude, or any other reason. No matter their motive, Jesus was addressing their pride.

Jesus does not say to guess what place you should be at, which would still make the invitee think about himself and his honor among guests. If we were to guess our place wrong, that would bring shame to us. Even if we guessed our place right, it would still lead to a prideful attitude because we are thinking about ourselves and what we have done to earn that place.

Jesus says to take the lowest place no matter what. Jesus is addressing the heart of a man that we should not exalt ourselves. If we are humble and take the lowest position, we are exalted by being asked to move up in place. If we are never moved from the lowest place, which Jesus doesn't address but is possible, we are humbled that we are in the lowest place and avoid any shame of being moved down. Either way, we have the mind of Christ, in which He made Himself of no reputation and humbled Himself. Because of this humbleness, God highly exalted Him and gave Him the Name which is above every name (Philippians 2:7-9).

So whether you are invited to a wedding feast or anywhere else in life, be humble as Christ is humble.

Provoked though

Whoever exalts himself will be humbled, and he who humbles himself will be exalted.

Chapter 44

The Parable of the Dinner Host

Luke 14:12-14

Audience

Invitees at the house of one of the rulers of the Pharisees (Luke 14:1).

Prompt

Jesus healed a man who had dropsy after asking the dinner invitees if it was lawful to heal on the Sabbath (Luke 14:2-6). He then spoke this parable immediately after the parable of the wedding invitees.

Explanation

After addressing how to think about being a invitee, Jesus now addresses the host of the dinner with this parable. He tells him not to invite anyone to a dinner, friends, family, rich neighbors, or whoever is capable of repaying. Instead, he should invite those who have no means to repay: the poor, maimed, lame, and blind. This will bless the host and the payment for this action will happen at the resurrection of the just.

Jesus is addressing the same self-exalting attitude that he addressed in the previous parable except now the subject is the host instead of the invited. Jesus is not saying that you cannot ever have a feast with your friends, relatives, or neighbors. He had the Passover supper with His disciples who were His friends. He is talking about the motive of why certain people are invited. If you are inviting those who can repay you in some way to gain their favor and eventually be repaid, you are throwing a feast for the wrong reason.

If you are inviting those who cannot repay, you are humbling yourself in the same way you would humble yourself by taking the lowest place at a wedding. Not only will you bless those who cannot repay, but you will be blessed yourself. Jesus doesn't explain what the blessing will be, but blessings for doing good to others can take many forms. Furthermore, by inviting those who cannot repay, you will earn rewards at the resurrection of the just that will last for eternity.

Provoked thought

Do good to those who cannot repay you, for you will be blessed and earn eternal rewards.

Chapter 45

The Parable of the Wise Steward

Luke 16:1-8

Audience
The parable is directed at the disciples (Luke 16:1) but the Pharisees also heard it (Luke 16:14).

Prompt
This parable follows the parables of the lost sheep, the lost coin, and lost son after the Pharisees and scribes complained, saying, "This Man receives sinners and eats with them" (Luke 15:2).

Explanation
A rich man had a steward that was accused of wasting his goods. The rich man required an account of his stewardship because he would not let him be his steward any longer. The steward thought of other jobs he might do but did not want to do them. He decided to make friends with his master's debtors so they would receive him after he was no longer a steward. He took two of the debtors' bills and lowered the amount they owed. The rich man commended the steward for dealing wisely.

This parable is about using money wisely. When the steward knew he would be kicked out of his stewardship, he made friends with others through lowering the amount they owed.

The debtors probably saw this as an act of kindness and would at least be friendly to the steward because of it. The unjust steward used money to make friends.

Jesus comments after the parable, "For the sons of this world are more shrewd (wise) in their generation than the sons of light" (Luke 16:8). Unbelievers know how to make friends with their money. They regard money very highly because it can be their master (Luke 16:13).

Believers should not serve money, but that doesn't mean we don't use it wisely. In fact, Proverbs 19:4 says "wealth makes many friends." Jesus echos this proverb in Luke 16:9 by saying, "make friends for yourselves with unrighteous mammon, that when you fail, they may receive you into an everlasting home." Since money makes friends, friends will receive us when we fail. The "everlasting home" we are received into is a home that is built on faith in God that will last beyond the earthly trouble that has caused us to fail.

Fail in the passage does not necessarily mean go bankrupt, but when we need help, they are there to help us. Why is mammon/money unrighteous? Because it has no moral quality. Money itself is not bad; it's "morality" is determined by the heart of the user. Believers should be generous with their money because it makes friends that will help in times of need.

Provoked thought
Make friends for yourselves with unrighteous money, that when you fail, they may receive you into an everlasting home.

Chapter 46

The Parable of the Barren Fig Tree

Luke 13:6-9

Audience

"Some" in a crowd (Luke 13:1).

Prompt

After being told about Galileans whose blood Pilate had mingled with Roman sacrifices, Jesus talks to His audience about who is a worse sinner (Luke 13:2). We are not told what His audience said about the Galileans, but there must have been an angle of self-righteousness prompting Jesus' response that equates the audience as being of the same "level" of sinner if they do not repent (Luke 13:15).

Explanation

Jesus tells this parable to illustrate how God deals with unfruitful people. In the parable, a man looks for fruit on a fig tree that is three years old. The man expects there to be fruit after this time and finds none. He orders the keeper of his vineyard to cut the tree down. The keeper asks for one more year to take care of the tree. If the tree bears fruit after that time, the tree will be kept. But if not, he will cut it down as ordered.

Before this parable, Jesus says that two groups, the Galileans in the prompt and eighteen others on whom the tower of Siloam fell, are not worse sinners than other men even though they were killed. The Jews seemed to generally have the attitude that if something bad happened to you, it was caused by your sin (John 9:2). Bad happenings can be a direct result of sinning, but sometimes they happen so "the works of God should be revealed" (John 9:3).

In the parable, the keeper of the vineyard wants to do everything he can to create the conditions for the fig tree to produce fruit. If he does everything correctly, such as fertilize, water, and make sure there is proper sunlight, and the tree still does not produce fruit, then he knows it is the tree that is bad and not the circumstances. God treats us in a similar manner, both disciples and unbelievers.

God desires all men to be saved (1 Timothy 2:3-4). God did everything He could to save us by making salvation free; the only requirement is faith in Jesus Christ (which is not a work). God has also made Himself understandable to His creation so that we are without excuse in knowing Who God is (Romans 1:20). Putting these things together, God gives every single person opportunities in their life to believe in His Son and also has empowered everyone with the ability to believe (those with mental disabilities that do not allow them to believe are another topic outside this book). Therefore, just as the keeper in the vineyard, God has made the circumstances right. If someone does not believe, they are a "bad tree."

For believers, God wants all of us to grow in grace and knowledge and walk in good works (2 Peter 3:18, Ephesians 2:8-10). We have the Bible, which gives us the right circumstances for sanctification (John 17:17). But if we do not bear fruit, as the fig tree did not, we will be "cut down." This does not mean we lose our salvation or we were never saved at all; it only means we are not useful, and God will not use us in His work. It is also worth noting that we are only to bear fruit, not produce it. God's job is to produce the fruit. We are only told to abide in Him so that we can be used by God and bear His fruit (John 15:1-8). Even if we stop bearing fruit, God is always willing to use us again if we confess our sins and come back into fellowship with Him (1 John 1:6-9). What a great promise that God will always receive us again!

This parable could also be applied to a group of believers that are participating in a ministry. If that ministry is not fruitful, God will "cut it down" and not use it anymore. The ministry could cease as an organization or still exist but no longer be doing God's work.

Instead of applying this parable to the individual level, Jesus could also be speaking to the nation of Israel as a whole. Since He preceded this parable with the words, "unless you repent you will all likewise perish" (Luke 13:5) after being told of literal deaths of groups of Jews, Jesus could be hinting at 70 AD, in which Jerusalem was destroyed and many Jews were killed. Israel was "cut down" like the barren fig tree and many also literally died like the Galileans and the group at the tower of Siloam.

I think each applications, individuals, groups, and the nation of Israel, could be argued for when explaining this parable. Since we as the Church are not Israel, we cannot apply this parable to whatever nation we live in, but only at the individual or group level. Ultimately, Jesus' point is that if we are not fruitful, whether individually, as a group, or Israel, God will not use us for His purposes.

Provoked thought

If we are not bearing fruit, God will not use us for His purposes.

Chapter 47

The Parable of the Praying Pharisee and Tax Collector

Luke 18:9-14

Audience
Some who trusted in themselves that they were righteous and despised others (Luke 18:9).

Prompt
Jesus most likely noticed the behavior of the audience, but it is not clear whether they were interacting with Jesus.

Explanation
A Pharisee and a tax collector were praying at the temple. The Pharisee prayed with himself that he was not like other sinners and then promoted his own works. The tax collector, who stood afar off, would not even look to heaven but beat his breast, saying, "God, be merciful to me a sinner!"

The Pharisee thought he was praying to God, but in reality he was only talking to himself (Luke 18:11). The Pharisee did not humble himself before a holy God but instead exalted himself above other men. As verse 9 says, he trusted in himself and because of that he despised others. Pride will end in destruction (Proverbs 16:18).

On the other hand, the tax collector humbled himself, not

regarding himself worthy to even look in the direction of heaven. He knew he was a sinner and his justification rested on God's mercy and not his own works.

Those who exalt themselves will be humbled at the final judgment (Revelation 20:11-12) and often during their earthly life (Proverbs 13:15). Those who humble themselves will be exalted in heaven because through faith in Christ they have overcome the world (1 John 4:5).

We should never think we are worthy before God because of anything we do but only humble ourselves in recognition of His holiness.

Provoked thought
Everyone who exalts himself will be humbled, and he who humbles himself will be exalted.

Chapter 48

The Parable of the Servant's Duties

Luke 17:7-9

Audience

The disciples (Luke 17:1).

Prompt

The apostles asked Jesus to increase their faith (Luke 17:5). Jesus explained if they had faith as a mustard seed, as an example, they could move a mulberry tree (Luke 17:6).

Explanation

Jesus asks the disciples if they had a servant who tended sheep or plowed the field, would they ask the servant when they came in from the field to sit down and eat? The master would say to him, "Prepare something for my supper, and gird yourself and serve me till I have eaten and drunk and afterward you will eat and drink." The master would not thank the servant for doing what he was commanded.

Before telling this parable, Jesus indicated that it is not the quantity of faith we have that matters. The disciples could do amazing things, like move trees, with a very small amount of faith. I believe Jesus is pointing out that it is not the quantity but the object of our faith that matters. This parable is explaining how to understand and apply the faith that we have.

A master does not thank his servant for doing the duties he is assigned. This may sound a bit strange to us but if God is our Master, it aligns with His character. Since He has already prepared beforehand our good works (Ephesians 2:10), we are not able to do anything that He hasn't already "assigned" to us. Furthermore, God also does not need us to do anything because He could accomplish His will without us. In this way, we are unprofitable servants who only did what was our duty (Luke 17:10). None of our works will impress God.

Masters should be thankful of any servant they have and treat them well (Colossians 4:1), but the focus of this parable is on disciples of Jesus being servants. We should not ask for an increase in faith because faith as small as a mustard seed is sufficient. We should recognize what we have been commanded to do and pray for the ability to complete the task. In this way we will recognize our place as unprofitable servants who only accomplished what we were commanded.

This mindset humbles us before God, helping us learn our place in His creation. He will reward us for our work, but in the end, we cannot do anything other than what He prepared. I pray that we would understand what God has commanded us to do in whatever state of life we are in and accomplish those works for Him.

Provoked thought

When we have done all those things which we were commanded, say, "We are unprofitable servants. We have done what was our duty to do."

Chapter 49

The Parable of a Friend at Midnight

Luke 11:5-8

Audience

The disciples (Luke 11:1-2).

Prompt

One of the disciples asked Jesus to teach them to pray, "as John also taught his disciples" (Luke 11:1). This parable follows Luke's account of the disciples' prayer, more popularly called the Lord's prayer (Luke 11:2-4).

Explanation

This is the first of two parables in Jesus' discourse of teaching the disciples to pray.

The disciples are to imagine that they go to a friend at midnight. They ask for three loaves of bread for they need to serve a friend of theirs who arrived at their house. Their friend will answer them, "Do not trouble me; the door is now shut, and my children are with me in bed; I cannot rise and give to you." But if they persist in asking, the friend will give them the bread they need not because of their friendship but because of their persistence.

This parable is about persistence in asking for something. Jesus just taught the disciples how to pray and in that prayer He told them to ask for four things: daily bread, forgiveness of sins, not leading into temptation, and deliverance from the evil one (Luke 11:3-4). Given that Jesus says "daily" bread, we should pray for these things at least daily. However, in the parable, the man does not leave his friend until he gets the bread. Therefore, we should continually pray for things as often as we can until we receive them.

God may not give us what we pray for right away, such as waiting to avenge us (Luke 18:7). He also may say no to our request, which means we were praying for the wrong thing (James 4:3). But if we are persistent in asking, He will give us what we need. Notice in the parable that the friend gave the man "as many as he needs," not necessarily as many as he wanted.

For example, if we pray for wisdom we know that God will give to us "liberally and without reproach" (James 1:5). But He may give it to us by putting us through a trial, which we probably didn't pray for (James 1:2). This trial will give us the wisdom we needed but maybe not the wisdom we wanted; maybe we aren't ready for certain wisdom because we don't have wisdom that is a predecessor to what we want. But God will continue to give us what we ask for because of our persistence.

Provoked thought
Be persistent in asking and it will be given to you.

Chapter 50

The Parable of a Father Giving to a Son

Luke 11:11-13

Audience

The disciples (Luke 11:1-2).

Prompt

One of the disciples asked Jesus to teach them to pray, "as John also taught his disciples" (Luke 11:1). This parable follows Luke's account of the disciples' prayer, more popularly called the Lord's prayer (Luke 11:2-4), the parable of the friend at midnight, and Jesus' explanation of asking, seeking, and knocking (Luke 11:9-10).

Explanation

While the parable of the friend at midnight explained how often we should pray for things, this parable talks about the kind of gift(s) we will receive when we ask.

If a son would ask his father for bread, would the father give him a stone? If the son asks for a fish, will the father give him a serpent? If the son asks for an egg, will the father offer a scorpion? The implied answer to all of these questions is "Of course not!" If men, being evil, know how to give good gifts to their children, how much more will God give the Holy Spirit to those who ask Him!

Man has a sinful nature that is "deceitful above all things and desperately wicked" (Jeremiah 17:9). God, on the other hand, is completely just and holy (Deuteronomy 32:4, Isaiah 6:3). This parable compares the giving of man and God from the lesser to the greater.

When a son asks a father for something useful or good, a father would not give him something useless or harmful. Jesus is not saying this could never happen, because certainly there are fathers who do not always give good gifts to their children. He is making a statement that even a father with the sin nature, which is every single one, is capable of giving good gifts to their children.

Compared to God, how much better are the gifts He will give! The ultimate gift is the Holy Spirit Who is able to guide us into all truth (John 16:13). God gives the Holy Spirit and the Holy Spirit in turn gives more specific gifts, such as wisdom and knowledge (1 Corinthians 12:4-7). By this parable, it seems that after God gives the Holy Spirit, the Holy Spirit is the Mediator of giving gifts to men which parallels 1 Corinthians 12:11. It is beyond the scope of this book to discuss the intricacies of the Holy Spirit's gifts, but at least we can say the Holy Spirit has a part in gift giving.

Because God is all good, He is incapable of giving evil or bad gifts as men are. Even a gift we perceive to be bad, such as the thorn in the flesh Paul experienced, is for our good. The thorn was clearly painful in some way because Paul asked for it to be taken away three times (Paul had persistence in asking!). But God said no and gave Paul the gift he needed, which was the understanding that the thorn was to keep him from exalting himself above measure (2 Corinthians 12:7-10). May we also see

God's perspective on gifts we receive from Him, always giving us what we need.

Provoked thought

If people, being evil, know how to give good gifts to their children, how much more will your heavenly Father give the Holy Spirit to those who ask Him.

Chapter 51

The Parable of the Two Debtors

Luke 7:41-43

Audience

Dinner guests of a Pharisee, disciples, and the sinful woman (Luke 7:36, 37, 40).

Prompt

Jesus directed this parable to Simon Peter in response to the judgemental attitude of the Pharisee who invited Him to dinner. The Pharisee was judging Jesus for allowing the woman to wash His feet (Luke 7:39).

Explanation

Jesus told Simon the story of a creditor with two debtors. One debtor owed the creditor five hundred denarii and the other fifty. Neither had any means to repay, but the creditor freely forgave both. Jesus asked Simon which debtor loved the creditor more. Simon answered correctly the one who owed more and was forgiven.

Jesus uses this parable to contrast the sinful woman's attitude against the Pharisee's. Jesus told the parable to Simon, but obviously it was meant for everyone at the meal to hear. A denarii was one day of wages, so the one debtor in the parable owed over a year's worth of wages and the other owed a little less than two months. A person forgiven of a lot of debt will love the forgiver more than one who only has little debt.

The sinful woman, who had many sins (Luke 7:47), was forgiven of them all because of her faith (Luke 7:50). She loved Jesus, the Forgiver, by washing His feet with her tears, drying them with her hair, kissing His feet, and anointing them with oil. Her sinful works created a lot of debt (Romans 4:4). The Pharisee, who did not believe he had to be forgiven of much if anything, did not do any of these things.

No one can pay the debt that we owe God (Romans 3:20), but He freely forgives us just like the creditor in the parable. The word in Luke 7:42 translated "freely forgave" means "to give a favor." That is what grace is: favor. Since there is no way we can pay our debt, the favor we receive from God cannot be earned. It must be unearned or unmerited. Faith is the only way we can receive salvation by grace from God, "for all have sinned an fall short of the glory of God, being justified freely by His grace through the redemption that is in Christ Jesus" (Romans 3:23-24).

Even though some of us may have a larger "sin debt" than others, we should all love Jesus for forgiving us. Since none of us could pay the debt, our love for Him should be very great. Notice also the sinful woman's love was not a feeling, but action. John 3:16 says, "For God so loved the world that He gave His only begotten Son, that whoever believes in Him should not perish but have everlasting life." And "if God so loved us, we also ought to love one another" (I John 4:11). Let us "do" love because we have been forgiven such a great debt.

Provoked thought

To whom much is forgiven, the same loves much. To whom little is forgiven, the same loves little.

Chapter 52

The Parable of the Compassionate Samaritan
Luke 10:30-37

Audience
A lawyer (Luke 10:25) but the disciples were mostly likely present as well (Luke 10:23).

Prompt
The lawyer asked Jesus, "Who is my neighbor?" after asking, "What must I do to inherit eternal life?"

Explanation
The lawyer was testing Jesus when he asked Him about inheriting eternal life (Luke 10:25). Jesus would have known that and answered him with a question about what he thought the law said about inheriting eternal life. The man quoted Deuteronomy 6:5 and Leviticus 19:18. Jesus affirmed his answer that if he followed those commandments he would inherit eternal life.

Why is Jesus affirming a works-based path to get into heaven? Technically, a person could get into heaven if he never sinned; therefore Jesus' answer to the lawyer is correct. The problem is that it is not possible for man to not sin. That is why faith in Jesus Christ is the only option to enter heaven. Jesus answered this way because the lawyer was testing Him. We should not build a doctrine of works- based salvation based on this verse because Jesus is testing the lawyer just as he is testing Jesus.

The lawyer wanted to justify himself and his works so he asked, "Who is my neighbor?" Jesus now had an opportunity to show the lawyer the intent of the law by telling the parable of the compassionate Samaritan.

A man was traveling to Jericho from Jerusalem when thieves attacked him, stripped him of his clothing, wounded him, and left him half dead. A priest and Levite walked by the man and passed by on the other side of the road. A Samaritan came and had compassion on the man. He dressed his wounds, put him on his animal, and took care of him when he arrived at an inn. The next day he gave the innkeeper two denarii, telling him to take care of the man and that if more money was required, he would repay him. The parable ends with a question to the lawyer: "So which of these three do you think was neighbor to him who fell among the thieves?" The lawyer correctly answered the Samaritan who showed mercy.

For being a relatively long parable, the simple provoked thought is about showing compassion to everyone for everyone is your neighbor. The word translated "mercy" in verse 37 can also be translated "compassion." The priest and the Levite, who were supposed to be the ones who followed the law, passed by the robbed man. They were not following Leviticus 19:18. The Samaritan (the Samaritans were hated by the Jews) did show compassion on the man and took care of him. He even paid for the time needed for the robbed man to rest and recover at an inn. The Samaritan did all of this without knowing who the man was.

When Jesus asked who was the robbed man's neighbor, the

lawyer knew it was the Samaritan and answered rightly. Jesus says, "Go and do likewise."

In order to love your neighbor, there must be some sacrifice of time, resources, or energy to help him with no expectation of benefit or repayment to the one who helps. The Samaritan had this compassion and we should "go and do likewise."

Provoked thought
Love your neighbor by showing compassion to everyone.

Chapter 53

The Parable of
the Animal Fallen in a Pit

Matthew 12:11, Luke 14:5

Audience
In Luke, the audience is the Pharisee's dinner party (Luke 14:1).

In Matthew, the audience is anyone in the synagogue including Pharisees (Matthew 12:9-10).

Prompt
In Luke, Jesus asked the Pharisees if it is lawful to heal on the Sabbath before healing a man with dropsy.

In Matthew, the Pharisees tried to accuse Jesus by asking Him if it is lawful to heal on the Sabbath.

Explanation
Jesus uses this parable to compare healing on the Sabbath to helping an animal. Jesus asked the Pharisees if they would pull a donkey, a sheep, or an ox out of a pit if they fell in on the Sabbath. The implied answer is yes. Exodus 23:5 even says to help in this situation, and there is no restriction on whether it can be done on the Sabbath or not.

The Pharisees could not answer the parable because they knew if they answered yes to the question they would look like fools for helping animals but not people on the Sabbath. Jesus is making the point that people are more important than animals. If animals can be saved, then certainly people can be healed.

But the larger point Jesus is making is the problem with the man-made rules the Pharisees had created regarding the Sabbath. Their rules hindered the original intent of the Sabbath, which was to give men rest (Exodus 20:10). The Sabbath was made for man to give him rest as a holy day. Man was not made for the Sabbath to adhere to a strict set of rules (Mark 2:27). If that rest was interrupted by a crisis that had to be solved, such as taking care of an animal or healing a man, the actions of solving the crisis did not make the day unholy.

God desires mercy and not sacrifice (Matthew 12:7, Hosea 6:6). Doing good on the Sabbath is showing mercy while the man-made rules the Pharisees had created were sacrifice. Mercy or doing good is holiness that remembers the Sabbath and keeps it holy (Exodus (20:8), while the rules were sacrifices that had an appearance of holiness but were not done with a merciful heart, especially when it hindered good. Therefore the law supported doing good on the Sabbath.

How wonderful that God's laws are always in our best interest and seek the best for us rather than a God who creates rules only for rules' sake. We in the Church are not under the law of Moses, including the law of the Sabbath (Galatians 3:25). This parable about the Sabbath is not directly applicable to us. However, we are under the law of Christ (I Corinthians 9:21) and have the same parallel between mercy and sacrifice. When we follow the law of Christ, those laws always bring us into a closer relationship with Him and sanctify us (I Thessalonians 4:1-3). Our desire should be the substance of Christ (Colossians 2:17). We need to understand the intent of the commands which God gave us rather than following regulations which only have the appearance of religion (Colossians 2:23).

Provoked thought

It is lawful to do good on the Sabbath.

Chapter 54

The Parable of Building a Tower

Luke 14:28-30

Audience
Great multitudes (Luke 14:25).

Prompt
Jesus is teaching the multitudes about what it means to be a disciple of His.

Explanation
Jesus tells this parable in the form of a question. If they intend to build a tower, they would first sit down and count the cost to decide whether they have the resources to finish it. Counting the cost would avoid the shame of laying the foundation and not finishing. If the tower was incomplete, mockers would come and say, "This man began to build and was not able to finish."

If we are to be a disciple of Jesus, we count the cost of following Him just as man would do before building a tower. If we are to count the cost of being a disciple, it is more than money; it is the focus of our life. It includes our time and resources, but also a mindset which excludes actions that do not "build our tower" or are part of being a disciple. This is what Jesus means by "bearing our cross" in Luke 14:27. Counting the cost is looking at our time, resources, and energy and seeing if we can carry the cross we will be given when we come after Jesus.

As a point of clarification, counting the cost to bear a cross is a matter of discipleship, not "believer-ship." All God tells you to do to be saved is believe in Jesus Christ who paid the penalty for your sins. In this passage, Jesus is talking about discipleship which happens after you are saved. Once you are a believer, you are to count the cost if you desire to be a disciple and come after Christ. This passage is about sanctification not justification.

Just as someone is mocked for not finishing a tower, we can be mocked for not carrying on as a disciple. Many believers are mocked when they sin and the world loves to do it. Sometimes believers give up on being a disciple as the parable of the sower makes clear. However, we should strive to be a disciple to the end of our lives and "finish the tower." Even though we cannot be a perfect disciple while on this earth because we still sin as believers (Romans 7:14-25), we should not give up on discipleship. If we sin or give up discipleship, God will always welcome us back when we confess our sins (I John 1:9). Better to finish the tower even though there may be gaps with no progress than to not finish at all.

Provoked thought
Whoever does not bear his cross and come after Jesus cannot be His disciple.

Chapter 55

The Parable of a King Making War

Luke 14:31-32

Audience

Great multitudes (Luke 14:25).

Prompt

Jesus teaches the multitudes about what it means to be a disciple of His. This parable follows the parable of building a tower.

Explanation

This parable is another picture of the cost of discipleship. Immediately after finishing the parable of building a tower, Jesus uses the word "or." This is signifying the same provoked thought using a different comparison.

The parable is in the form of a question to the audience as if they were a king making war against another king. Before making war, a king would consider if his outmatched forces can overcome the other king's army. If he cannot overcome the king, he would send a delegation for peace.

The king in this parable is forsaking all that he has against the invading army. If he believes he can defeat the other king, his entire army will be called upon to fight. If he believes he will lose, he will forsake any attempt of fighting and work out conditions for peace. Either way, he is counting the cost of before he does anything. He will "bear his cross" for whichever decision he makes. If he rushes into battle and loses, he will lose his entire kingdom.

Similarly, if we rush into discipleship without counting the cost, we will mostly likely end up like the seeds that fell on thorny soil in the parable of the sower. We may start off well, but we will wither in our commitment to being a disciple.

The king's entire kingdom rests on his planning and decision to meet the opposing king. How effective our discipleship is rests on how we are bearing our cross (Luke 14:27) and if we are forsaking everything (Luke 14:26, 33). Jesus says if we don't do these things we cannot be His disciple. I pray that we understand what it takes to be a disciple, properly counting the cost and then being productive.

Provoked thought
Whoever does not bear his cross and come after Jesus cannot be His disciple. Whoever does not forsake all that he has cannot be Jesus' disciple.

Chapter 56

The Parable of the Lost Sheep

Matthew 18:12-13, Luke 15:3-7

Audience

In Luke, Jesus is speaking to great multitudes (Luke 14:25), including tax collectors, sinners, Pharisees, and scribes (Luke 15:1-2).

In Matthew, Jesus is speaking to His disciples (Matthew 18:1), but there were probably more people around because a little child was close enough for Jesus to call him (Matthew 18:2).

Prompt

In Luke, after using parables to explain discipleship to Himself (Luke 14:25-35), the Pharisees and scribes complained, saying, "This Man receives sinners and eats with them" (Luke 15:2).

In Matthew, the disciples asked Jesus, "Who is the greatest in the kingdom of heaven?" (Matthew 18:1). Jesus answers by setting a child in their midst (Matthew 18:2) and saying, "whoever humbles himself as this little child is the greatest in the kingdom of heaven" (Matthew 18:3). This parable is told after Jesus warns the disciples not to despise children, "for the Son of Man has come to save that which was lost" (Matthew 18:10-11).

Explanation

Jesus told this parable two separate times with two different contexts. In Luke's telling, after talking about discipleship, the tax collectors and sinners drew near to Jesus, indicating they wanted to be disciples or at least were intrigued by what He said whereas the Pharisees and scribes complained about who Jesus was drawing to Himself. In Matthew's telling, Jesus tells this parable to explain how Jesus is seeking lost persons.

Jesus' audience is supposed to imagine they have a hundred sheep. If one goes missing, the natural thing to do is leave the ninety-nine and look for the lost sheep. When the sheep is found, of course you would rejoice! In fact, you would rejoice more about finding the lost sheep than about the ninety-nine who were never lost. After coming home, you would want the joy to be spread among your friends and neighbors that the lost sheep has been found.

This is a very relatable parable because we all lose things. We can all agree that when something is lost, we are not joyful because of all the things that are not lost. Joy comes when we find what we lost. If we have the means to find it, normally we will search for it until it is found. It is also very typical that when we find it, we tell other people because we are so joyful it is no longer lost.

In Luke's telling, the provoked thought is focused on comparing the joy that is experienced after finding something lost to the joy of having what is not lost. Matthew's telling makes it clear that Jesus is the One who is seeking what is lost, but we can still ascertain the same from the context in Luke that Jesus is seeking those who will draw near to Him (tax collectors and sinners).

Just as there is joy over finding a lost sheep, there is more joy in heaven when a sinner (all of us) repents, or changes their mind and believes in Jesus than just or righteous persons who need no repentance. The just persons Jesus is talking about could be the Pharisees and scribes because they thought they were just and did not need to change their mind about Jesus to get into heaven. In this case, Jesus is being sarcastic about them being just. Their complaining prompted this parable, and it makes sense that Jesus could be describing their self-righteousness in which they thought they didn't need repentance.

The just persons could also be saved people who don't need repentance because they already repented and were given eternal life. Believers still need to change their mind about sinning after they are saved, but the purpose of this repentance is to restore fellowship with God, not to get into heaven. Either way, there is the most joy in heaven when a person believes in Jesus. What a wonderful thing to know all of heaven erupts in joy when a person believes in Jesus!

In Luke's telling the man seeking the sheep looks for it until he finds it (Luke 15:4). In Matthew, Jesus says, "if he should find it" (Matthew 18:13). Why the difference? We know that God desires all men to be saved (1 Timothy 2:4) but we also know not all men will be saved (Revelation 20:15). How can both be true? This parable reconciles this seeming contradiction.

Jesus is seeking all those who are lost that they may be saved by believing in Him. However, as the parable makes clear, it is not guaranteed that He will "find" all those who are lost. Why? Because God has given us the ability to choose and we must repent (change our mind) in order to be saved (Luke 15:7). Therefore the "finding" of a lost person does not rest completely on the "Seeker" or Jesus. If it was, everyone would be "found" because that is God's will (Matthew 18:14). That which is lost (people) also have a responsibility in the seeking process, which is to believe in Jesus as Savior.

Since it is not God's will that any should perish (2 Peter 3:9), we can be certain that Jesus is doing everything He can to seek and save us. We can rest in this fact, because often times we are challenged by situations in life where we can say, "Why didn't God do something about that?" or "How could God not give them a chance to believe in Jesus?" We may not understand His actions, but we can be sure that He did everything He could to seek and save that which was lost.

Whenever these faith-stretching situations happen, we must not forget that people have a responsibility to respond to God's seeking. When we get to heaven and if God allows us to look back at situations in earthly life, we'll understand His perspective and all the things He did to seek everyone that none should perish.

Provoked thought
Matthew: The Son of Man has come to save that which was lost.

Luke: There is more joy in heaven over one sinner who repents than over ninety-nine just persons who need no repentance.

Chapter 57

The Parable of
the Lost Coin

Luke 15:9-10

Audience

Jesus is speaking to great multitudes (Luke 14:25), including tax collectors, sinners, Pharisees, and scribes (Luke 15:1-2).

Prompt

This parable directly follows the parable of the lost sheep, after the Pharisees and scribes complained, saying, "This Man receives sinners and eats with them" (Luke 15:2).

Explanation

The parable of the lost coin is a similar scenario to the parable of the lost sheep. A woman possessing ten coins loses one. She cleans her house and searches carefully until she finds the coin. When she finds it, she calls her friends and neighbors together and tells them to rejoice with her, for the lost coin has been found.

The parable makes clear that just as we rejoice with friends and neighbors when we find something that is lost, the angels rejoice with each other when a sinner repents or changes their mind and believes. We know angels desire to look into things related to the Gospel (1 Peter 1:12) and they are ministering spirits sent to those who will inherit salvation (Hebrews 1:14). We don't know the details, but in some way angels understand the Gospel and are ministering or serving us who inherit salvation. I believe the text allows this ministering to happen before and after we believe, which means they are active in their ministry to us throughout our whole lives. What a neat thought to know that angels tell each other, "The person I am ministering to just believed," and they all rejoice! Or maybe all the angels know when a person believes because there is some sort of announcement. Either way, no wonder they rejoice because they have been involved in us coming to Christ!

Do you think the angel or angels ministering to you just told the other angels and rejoiced, although not as much as when a sinner believes, that we just figured out they communicate their joy to each other?

Provoked thought
There is joy in the presence of the angels of God over one sinner who repents.

Chapter 58

The Parable of
the Lost Son
Luke 15:11-32

Audience
Jesus is speaking to great multitudes (Luke 14:25), including tax collectors, sinners, Pharisees, and scribes (Luke 15:1-2).

Prompt
This parable follows the parables of the lost sheep and the lost coin, after the Pharisees and scribes complained saying, "This Man receives sinners and eats with them" (Luke 15:2).

Explanation
The parable of the lost son, sometimes called the prodigal son, is very popular and has received many interpretations over the years. But because it is a parable, it has one central point or provoked thought that Jesus is making to His audience. Let's summarize the parable, and then we will look into how it brings together the parables of the lost sheep and the lost coin.

The younger son of a man with two sons demanded his portion of the inheritance. Soon after his father divided the inheritance, the younger son journeyed to a far country and wasted everything with prodigal or riotous living. A famine came to the land, and because he had nothing, he gave himself to a citizen of that country and fed his pigs. He was not even given any food for himself. But he came to himself and realized his father's servants lived better than him. He resigned himself to apologize to his father and become one of his servants. Then he left for his father's house.

His father saw him coming and had compassion. He ran to his son, hugging and kissing him when he arrived. His son apologized and no longer considered himself worthy to be called his father's son. But his father threw a party in honor of his son's return.

The older brother, who was in the field, found out about the party and was angry. His father came to him and pleaded that he join the feast. The son summarized his service to his father and complained that he was never given a goat to throw a party with his friends but a feast is had for the younger brother after he returned from riotous living. The father explained it is right to be joyful, for his son was dead and is alive again, and was lost and is found.

When put in context of the other "lost" parables, the parable of the lost son is giving a more direct example to the audience about how to rejoice when a lost person is found. Jesus told two parables explaining the joy in heaven over sinners that repent; now He explains how this joy plays out on earth. It is certainly not wrong to read this parable and put ourselves in the place of one of the three main characters to see which attitude we have or apply the concept in other ways. However, It it not correct to say this parable is a model of how to get saved, interpret the details too far or incorrectly, or anything like that. The parable has a singular point and we should keep it in context with the two parables that preceded it.

The father has the right attitude to rejoice when his lost son returns. The son repented or changed his mind and humbled himself. The father has more joy over his son that was dead and is alive again and was lost and is found (notice the repetition of this phrase) than over his older son who was never lost.

It seems the older son thought the father had no joy over him. But when that father replies to the older son, he clearly is joyful that he has never left and says, "all that I have is yours" (Luke 15:31). Since the younger son repented, the father had the right and necessary joyful attitude which did not diminish any joy over the older son. But the older son had the incorrect attitude and was not joyful at all.

May we always be like the father and the angels who do not hold a grudge against anyone but are joyful when they are alive and found.

Provoked though
We should rejoice over sinners who repent, who were dead and are alive again, who were lost and now are found.

All Provoked Thoughts

The Parable of a Lamp on a Lampstand
Mark 4:21, Luke 8:16 & 11:33

1st telling: Take heed how you hear. For whoever has, to him more will be given; and whoever does not have, even what he seems to have will be taken from him.

2nd telling: Take heed that the light which is in you is not darkness.

Section 1: Mystery Kingdom Parables

The Parable of the Sower
Matthew 13:3-9 & 18-23, Mark 4:3-8, Luke 8:4-8 & 11-15

People will react differently to the message of the kingdom. Some will believe and some won't. Some that believe will produce fruit and some won't.

The Parable of the Wheat and Tares
Matthew 13:24-30 & 37-43

Believers and unbelievers will be together until the end of the age of law when they will be separated; believers will enter the kingdom and unbelievers will be cast into hell.

The Parable of the Growing Seed
Mark 4:26-29

God is the One preparing the kingdom and man has no part in it's preparation.

The Parable of the Mustard Seed
Matthew 13:31-32, Mark 4:30-32, Luke 13:18-19

The kingdom will grow to an enormous size compared to its very small beginning size.

The Parable of the Leaven
Matthew 13:33, Luke 13:20-21

The kingdom will permeate every part of life in every part of the world.

The Parable of the Hidden Treasure
Matthew 13:44

Jesus paid the purchase price for any Gentile to enter the kingdom of heaven.

The Parable of the Pearl of Great Price
Matthew 13:45-46

Jesus paid the purchase price for Israel to enter the kingdom of heaven.

The Parable of the Dragnet
Matthew 13:47-50

All peoples will be gathered before Jesus at the end of the tribulation; the wicked will be separated from the just and thrown into hell.

The Parable of the Householder
Matthew 13:52

To understand the kingdom, both new and old information must be put together.

Section 2: Kingdom Parables

The Parable of the Friends of the Bridegroom
Matthew 9:15, Mark 2:19-20, Luke 5:34-35
Since Jesus is present, it is a time of joy and not mourning.

The Parable of the New Cloth and Old Garment
Matthew 9:16, Mark 2:21, Luke 5:36
The joy that represents the Messiah's presence is incompatible with the mourning that represents the awaiting of His arrival.

The Parable of New and Old Wine and Wineskins
Matthew 9:17, Mark 2:22, Luke 5:37-38
Kingdom behaviors would be wasted before the kingdom appears.

The Parable of Old Wine
Luke 5:39
Kingdom conditions are better than pre-kingdom conditions.

The Parable of a Kingdom Divided
Matthew 12:25, Mark 3:24-25, Luke 11:17
Jesus cannot be casting out demons by Satan because that would render an end to Satan's kingdom.

The Parable of the Strong Man
Matthew 12:29, Mark 3:27, Luke 11:21-22
Jesus will plunder Satan's kingdom when the kingdom of God appears.

The Parable of the Great Supper
Luke 14:16-24
None of those men who were invited (Jewish religious leaders) shall taste God's supper (entrance into the kingdom).

The Parable of the Persistent Widow
Luke 18:1-8
Men always ought to pray and not lose heart.

The Parable of the Unforgiving Servant
Matthew 18:23-35
God will make us pay the consequences of our sin, if each of us, from our heart, does not forgive his brother.

The Parable of the Vineyard Workers
Matthew 20:1-16
The last will be first, and the first last. For many are called, but few chosen.

The Parable of the Two Sons
Matthew 21:28-32
Better to change your mind and do the will of the God than say you are doing His will and not do it.

The Parable of the Wicked Vinedressers
Matthew 21:33-44, Mark 12:1-12, Luke 20:9-16
The kingdom of God will be taken from the first century Jews and given to a nation (the tribulation Jews) bearing the fruits of it. Those who rejected the chief cornerstone will be judged.

The Parable of the Wedding for a King's Son
Matthew 22:1-14
Many are called, but few are chosen.

The Parable of the Master Returning from a Wedding
Luke 12:35-38
Be ready, for the Son of Man is coming at an hour you do not expect.

The Parable of the Fig Tree
Matthew 24:32-33, Mark 13:28-29, Luke 21:29-31
When you see all the events of the tribulation, know that Christ's second coming is near – at the doors!

The Parable of the Master Going Away
Mark 13:34
Take heed, watch and pray; for you do not know when the time of Jesus' return is.

The Parable of the Master and the Thief
Matthew 24:43, Luke 12:39
Be ready, for the Son of Man is coming at an hour you do not expect.

The Parable of the Wise and Evil Servants
Matthew 24:45-51, Luke 12:42-48
Matthew: A faithful and wise person will be watching and working while Jesus is delaying His coming but and evil person will not be watching and behaving badly. Both will be judged accordingly.

Luke: Everyone to whom much is given, from him much will be required; and to whom much has been committed, of him they will ask the more.

The Parable of the Ten Virgins
Matthew 25:1-13
Watch, for you know neither the day nor the hour in which the Son of Man is coming.

The Parable of the Talents
Matthew 25:14-30

To everyone who has, more will be given, and he will have abundance; but from him who does not have, even what he has will be taken away.

The Parable of the Minas
Luke 19:11-27

Everyone who has will be given; and from him who does not have, even what he has will be taken away from him.

Section 3: General Parables

The Parable of the Blind Leading the Blind
Luke 6:39

A man who cannot see clearly cannot correctly lead others and will lead himself and them into a bad situation.

The Parable of Pearls before Swine
Matthew 7:6

When you judge hypocritically, you are casting your character before men who can ruin you.

The Parable of the Good Tree, Good Fruit
Matthew 7:16-18 & 12:33, Luke 6:43-45

By their fruits you will know people's hearts, for out of the abundance of the heart the mouth speaks.

The Parable of the Wise and Foolish Men
Matthew 7:24-27, Luke 6:47-49

Hearing and doing Jesus' sayings provides a stable foundation in times of trouble. Hearing and not doing Jesus' sayings provides no foundation at all.

The Parable of the Children in the Marketplace
Matthew 11:16-17, Luke 7:31-32

The wise will prove what is correct by being wise. Wisdom is justified by all her children.

The Parable of the Rich Fool
Luke 12:16-21

Take heed and beware of covetousness, for one's life does not consist in the abundance of the things he possesses.

The Parable of the Wedding Invitees
Luke 14:7-11

Do good to those who cannot repay you, for you will be blessed and earn eternal rewards.

The Parable of the Dinner Host
Luke 14:12-14

Do good to those who cannot repay you, for you will be blessed and earn eternal rewards.

The Parable of the Wise Steward
Luke 16:1-8

Make friends for yourselves with unrighteous money, that when you fail, they may receive you into an everlasting home.

The Parable of the Barren Fig Tree
Luke 13:6-9

If we are not bearing fruit, God will not use us for His purposes.

The Parable of the Praying Pharisee and Tax Collector
Luke 18:9-14

Everyone who exalts himself will be humbled, and he who humbles himself will be exalted.

The Parable of the Servant's Duties
Luke 17:7-9

When we have done all those things which we were commanded, say, "We are unprofitable servants. We have done what was our duty to do."

The Parable of a Friend at Midnight
Luke 11:5-8

Be persistent in asking and it will be given to you.

The Parable of a Father Giving to a Son
Luke 11:11-13

If people, being evil, know how to give good gifts to their children, how much more will your heavenly Father give the Holy Spirit to those who ask Him.

The Parable of the Two Debtors
Luke 7:41-43

To whom much is forgiven, the same loves much. To whom little is forgiven, the same loves little.

The Parable of the Compassionate Samaritan
Luke 10:30-37

Love your neighbor by showing compassion to everyone.

The Parable of the Animal Fallen in a Pit
Matthew 12:11, Luke 14:5

It is lawful to do good on the Sabbath.

The Parable of Building a Tower
Luke 14:28-30

Whoever does not bear his cross and come after Jesus cannot be His disciple.

The Parable of a King Making War
Luke 14:31-32

Whoever does not bear his cross and come after Jesus cannot be His disciple. Whoever does not forsake all that he has cannot be Jesus' disciple.

The Parable of the Lost Sheep
Matthew 18:12-13, Luke 15:3-7

Matthew: The Son of Man has come to save that which was lost.

Luke: There is more joy in heaven over one sinner who repents than over ninety-nine just persons who need no repentance.

The Parable of the Lost Coin
Luke 15:9-10

There is joy in the presence of the angels of God over one sinner who repents.

The Parable of the Lost Son
Luke 15:11-32

We should rejoice over sinners who repent, who were dead and are alive again, who were lost and now are found.

About the author

Lucas is a bondservant of Jesus Christ.

Printed in the USA
CPSIA information can be obtained
at www.ICGtesting.com
LVHW091001250823
756265LV00020B/139